Michelle Kwan

Read all of the books in this exciting,
action-packed biography series!

Barry Bonds

Ichiro Suzuki

Lou Gehrig

Michelle Kwan

Mickey Mantle

Tim Duncan

SPORTS HEROES AND LEGENDS™

Michelle Kwan

by Anne E. Hill

LERNER
SPORTS
AN IMPRINT OF LERNER PUBLISHING GROUP

For Caleb—may all of your future dreams come true.
Love, Mommy

LernerSports
An imprint of Lerner Publishing Group
241 First Avenue North
Minneapolis, MN 55401 U.S.A.

Website address: www.lernerbooks.com

Cover photograph:
Rob Tringali/Sports Chrome

Library of Congress Cataloging-in-Publication Data

Hill, Anne E., 1974–
    Michelle Kwan / by Anne E. Hill.
        p.   cm. — (Sports heroes and legends)
    Includes bibliographical references and index.
        Contents: A dream come true—First steps—Family sacrifice—Finding Frank—Practice makes perfect—Taller and wiser—The best in the world—A hard landing—Chasing the gold—School days—On her own—Skating for joy.
        ISBN: 0–8225–1795–7 (lib. bdg. : alk. paper)
        1. Kwan, Michelle, 1980—Juvenile literature. 2. Skaters—United States—Biography—Juvenile literature. 3. Women skaters—United States—Biography—Juvenile literature. [1. Kwan, Michelle, 1980– 2. Ice skaters. 3. Chinese Americans—Biography. 4. Women—Biography.] I. Title. II. Series.
    GV850.K93H55 2004
    796.91'2'092—dc22   2003022797

Manufactured in the United States of America
1 2 3 4 5 6 – JR – 09 08 07 06 05 04

Contents

Prologue

A Dream Come True

As Michelle Kwan stepped onto the ice, the words of her coach, Frank Carroll, rang in her ears. "Go for it. Have fun." Michelle needed to hear these words of encouragement. Even though she had won the U.S. nationals in 1996 and was favored to win the gold medal at the 1998 nationals, a lot was riding on her performance. The three top-scoring women would travel to Nagano, Japan, to represent the United States at the Olympic Games. Skating in the Olympics had been seventeen-year-old Michelle's dream since she was a little girl.

But just weeks before nationals, it seemed like her dream might not come true. Michelle had injured her toe during a competition earlier in the skating season. Her doctor had ordered her to wear a hard cast for two weeks and then to wear a soft, removable cast and stay off the ice for four more weeks. Michelle had never been off the ice for more than two days

1

since she was five years old! She tried to stay positive and used the time off to focus on the basics of her skating technique.

With only five weeks to go until the nationals, Michelle still couldn't skate through her programs without mistakes, and some people advised her not to compete at nationals. She was one of the best female skaters in the United States, so the United States Figure Skating Association (USFSA) would probably allow her to compete on the Olympic team based on her previous record of wins. But Michelle wanted to earn her spot, not have it given to her.

Michelle worked closely with a physical therapist and was on the ice every day, practicing her routines. On Christmas Day, Michelle took a break with her family, and they all slept late and opened presents. Later in the day, Michelle got her biggest present when she cleanly landed a triple toe loop, one of the jumps most affected by her injury. In the triple toe loop, a skater uses a toe pick to take off backward and then makes three revolutions before landing on the same foot, still facing backward. Despite landing the toe loop, Michelle didn't have her usual consistency. She wasn't sure how she would do at nationals, but she knew she had to give it her best shot.

Backstage before she was scheduled to skate, Michelle felt the familiar mixture of nervousness and excitement run through her. She loves feeling the pressure of competition, and that night the pressure was definitely on. As she started skating, Michelle told herself to stay calm, and she focused on each element, or piece, of her program as it came. As her blades flew across the ice, her movements felt natural and easy. She landed each one of her jumps and finished the program with a huge grin on her face. The audience thundered their approval.

As she and Frank waited to hear her marks in the kiss-and-cry area (the place where skaters wait to see their scores), Michelle felt relieved and proud. Although they knew that her performance had been extremely strong, they were both astonished to see seven perfect 6.0s from the judges for presentation (the artistic part of the score).

Michelle couldn't have asked for a better beginning to nationals. To win the competition, she needed to hold on to her lead in the four-minute free skate (also called the long program) two days later. Even though the free skate counted for two-thirds of her overall score, Michelle wasn't nervous. She stepped onto the ice with a relaxed smile and took a deep breath before the music began. Throughout the program, the audience and the judges could see her confidence. She felt like she was floating as she effortlessly sailed through each of her jumps. As the time neared for the dreaded triple toe loop, Michelle remained calm. When she landed, there was a little pain, but she had done it! The audience—including Michelle's dad and sister—rose in a standing ovation. Although they didn't know it, they had just witnessed history being made. Michelle not only won the gold medal, she also scored eight more 6.0s for presentation. Her total of fifteen 6.0s for the two programs gave her the highest number of perfect scores ever awarded to a skater in a single competition. She'd overcome her injury and was on her way to the Olympics!

First Steps

When Michelle was born on July 7, 1980, in Torrance, California, the Kwan family included parents Danny and Estella as well as big brother Ron and big sister Karen. The Kwans were a supportive, hardworking family. They ran their own Chinese restaurant, the Golden Pheasant, in Torrance, which is just south of Los Angeles. The family spoke a mixture of English and Cantonese (Chinese) in the house.

When Michelle was a child, her father told her stories about growing up in a small village near the Chinese city of Canton (now called Guangzhou). Life was hard for his large family, and

Michelle's Chinese name is Kwan Wing Shan. She understands Chinese, but she doesn't speak it fluently.

there often wasn't enough to eat. Things got better when the Kwans moved to Hong Kong and eight-year-old Danny started going to school. There he met his classmate Estella, who was one of the best students in the class. Danny had a crush on Estella, but the two didn't start dating until many years later, after they had graduated from high school and had gone their separate ways.

Michelle's parents named her after the song "Michelle," by the Beatles. The song, which is Danny Kwan's favorite, tells the story of a boy who loves a girl with a beautiful name.

At age twenty-two, Danny moved to California and took two jobs—one as a cook and another with the Los Angeles telephone company. Estella remained in Hong Kong and worked as a nurse before becoming a television news anchorwoman. Danny returned to Hong Kong for a high school reunion, and he and Estella fell in love. After the couple married, Estella moved with Danny to California. They had Ron, Karen, and Michelle, who are each two years apart in age. Money was always tight, but the Kwans were happy.

Michelle has said that she doesn't remember much of her life before she started skating. She knows she liked to play with her stuffed animals and eat candy. She and Karen also took gymnastics lessons. Ron played hockey at the local skating rink, and soon Karen started skating there as well. Michelle wanted nothing more than to follow her brother and sister out onto the ice, but her parents insisted that at five years old, she was just too young. Michelle was a persistent child, and she didn't give up until she had convinced her parents to let her skate, too.

Michelle still remembers her first days skating at the rink at the local shopping mall in Rolling Hills Estates. "We wore rented brown skates that were ugly and stiff and hurt our feet, but we didn't care because we were having so much fun skating," she recalled. The Kwan sisters began taking group figure skating lessons. Their instructor taught them how to stand, how to hold on to the railing, and how to walk on the ice. They were even taught how to fall properly so they wouldn't hurt themselves. Michelle's ankles were weak, so she had trouble at first, but she was determined to succeed. She already loved the feeling of being on the ice. Just moving across the ice made her feel like she was flying.

❝I'm very lucky being the youngest in the family. I've always had someone to look out for me—thanks to my sister, Karen, and my brother, Ron.❞

—MICHELLE KWAN

Michelle and Karen were fast learners, and after six months of group lessons, they were ready to have private lessons. The sisters both loved skating and were eager to learn as much as they could. Michelle was impatient to move beyond stroking (pushing off on one foot) and gliding across the ice. She wanted to learn the jumps and spins that she saw older skaters perform. Michelle got her wish soon enough. Because she was so tiny, she had no trouble throwing herself into the air and completing a single turn before landing.

Michelle was born in the Chinese year of the monkey. Those born in the year of the monkey are known for being witty, artistic, and successful.

Before long Michelle and Karen were completely obsessed with skating. They started wearing their skating skirts to school and even slept in them! Most of Michelle's thoughts involved skating, and she often found herself daydreaming in class about the next time she could be on the ice, which would usually be later that day.

Michelle and Karen took private lessons several times a week. Danny and Estella could see that their daughters loved skating, and they also seemed to have natural talent for the sport, so the Kwans encouraged them to continue with it as long as they were having fun. At ages six and seven, Michelle couldn't imagine anything more fun than skating. She felt comfortable and free on the ice. Although she loved it, she had never thought about her future as a skater. Then she watched the 1988 Olympic Games on television, and everything changed.

Michelle was just seven and a half years old when American skater Brian Boitano won the gold medal in the men's figure skating competition, but she knew she was getting a glimpse into her own future. "It was like a thunderbolt struck," Michelle wrote in one of her books.

She vowed that one day she would go to the Olympics. She even started counting the years to see how old she would be at each of the upcoming Olympic Games. In 1994, she'd be thirteen; in 1998, seventeen; in 2002, twenty-one; and in 2006, she'd be twenty-five. Michelle vowed to be at each of these games. She didn't realize how hard it was to make the Olympic team. With her vivid imagination, she could see it all happening. She knew that one day she, too, would win an Olympic medal.

Michelle's motto for life and skating is: Work hard, be yourself, and have fun.

Chapter | Two

Family Sacrifice

Even though it may have seemed crazy for a little girl to know exactly what she wanted at such a young age, Michelle's parents took her Olympic dream seriously. Michelle and Karen wanted to keep skating and start competing. The two sisters had learned all they could from the instructors at the rink in Rolling Hills Estates. They needed a new coach who could teach them more complicated spins and jumps.

Danny found a teacher named Derek James at a nearby rink in Torrance. The girls started skating after school, after dinner, and even very early in the morning before school. To save time, Michelle and Karen would often sleep in their skating outfits so that they could just roll out of bed at 4:30 A.M., pile into the car, and head for the rink. "The only problem was, sleeping in skating tights is really uncomfortable," Michelle said. Still, the girls didn't complain.

They started competing in and winning local competitions.
Sometimes Karen won and sometimes Michelle took home the
trophy, but it seemed like almost every competition was won by
one of the two sisters. As the two continued competing, they
also began moving up in the ranks of the USFSA, which has
eight levels—pre-preliminary, preliminary, pre-juvenile, juve-
nile, intermediate, novice, junior, and senior. Each level has a
set of required elements. A skater must be able to perform these
elements in a test before advancing to the next level. When
skaters move to a new level, they receive a pin that signifies
they can compete with the other skaters at that level. All the
skaters who compete at the Olympics as well as the national
and world championships are senior-level skaters. Although
Michelle was anxious for the day she could be a senior lady, she
had to be patient and work her way up the ranks.

While the Kwans were prepared for the amount of work
involved, they hadn't expected skating to be so expensive. The

private lessons that both Karen and Michelle had almost every day, along with costumes and travel expenses for competitions, started to add up. Even though both Danny and Estella were working full time, it just wasn't enough. After the family ran out of money for lessons, the sisters skated without Derek for nine months. Instead of making Karen and Michelle cut back on their skating, however, Danny and Estella decided to sell their house and move into a house in Torrance owned by Danny's parents. Without any house payments, the Kwans had more money to contribute to skating. But they still had to make additional sacrifices. The sisters wore their cousins' hand-me-down clothes, bought used costumes and skates, and shared pairs of tights.

Skating was so expensive that Michelle's dad offered each of his daughters $50 a day *not* to skate as a way to save money. The girls loved skating so much that they didn't even consider the offer. Michelle skated through colds, sore throats, the flu, and even the chicken pox.

Michelle and Karen didn't mind sharing because they had grown to be best friends. Even though they were very different (Karen was more feminine and Michelle was a self-proclaimed tomboy), the two were inseparable on and off the ice. They knew what the other one was thinking and could often finish each other's sentences. "We were constantly talking," Michelle remembers. "In bed, at the rink . . . in the bathroom." In addition to being talented skaters, they excelled at school. Both were determined to get good grades. Despite the fact that they were only two years apart and often skated at the same level, the two never got competitive with each other. Karen was taller (she grew to be five-eight while Michelle is five-two) and thinner than Michelle. She was called "Big Kwan" while Michelle was known as "Little Kwan." They also had different skating styles. Michelle said that Karen skated like a ballerina, with elegance and grace. Michelle was more athletic and was known for her jumping and technique on the ice. The two knew each other's skating routines by heart and cheered for each other during competitions.

66 There are so many things I appreciate about my parents. They've always taught us about what's really important in life. Things like family and education and doing our best in everything. They've also sacrificed a lot to give my brother, sister, and me the opportunity to go after our dreams. 99

—MICHELLE KWAN

By the time Michelle was eleven and Karen was thirteen, the sisters had reached the junior level. Michelle knew that it was just a small step to the senior level, but she also knew that to make it as a senior, she needed more than five days a week on the ice. Unfortunately, the Torrance rink was busy with hockey players and recreational skaters on the weekends, so the Kwans couldn't practice then.

But Danny and Estella had another idea. They had friends who lived in a town a hundred miles away called Lake Arrowhead. Their friends told them that Lake Arrowhead was home to the famous Ice Castle Training Center, a state-of-the-art skating facility. The Kwans began driving the girls the long distance to Ice Castle so that they could skate on the weekends.

Ice Castle has two rinks, one open to the public and another for students of the school who are training with Ice Castle coaches. Michelle and Karen had to use the public rink because they weren't pupils at the school. Even at the public rink, however, the sisters were able to share the ice with talented skaters who were very serious about their sport. It was a far cry from the local rinks where Michelle was used to being one of the best skaters. Michelle said that at Ice Castle, "The more I learned, the more I saw that there was still so much to learn. It's like when you're . . . climbing up to a [mountain] ridge that you've been looking at for half the day, telling yourself, 'If I can just make it to the top, I'll be happy.' Then you get there only to see the rest of the mountain and how much farther you have to go."

But Michelle was committed. She wanted to go all the way to the top.

Chapter Three

Finding Frank

Michelle felt fortunate to be skating at Ice Castle, but she couldn't help wondering what it would be like to train there. Two of Michelle's idols, world champion Lu Chen and European champion Surya Bonaly, trained at the rink. Michelle hoped that one day she would be able to share the ice with them.

In the meantime, Michelle focused on the 1992 skating season. She won her first competition as a junior skater at the Southwest Pacific Regionals. Regionals are the first step for skaters who want to compete at the U.S. national championships. The top four regional finishers compete at sectionals against the winners from other regions in their section. The top four finishers in each section (there are three sections in the United States) qualify for nationals. Michelle's finish at regionals earned her a spot at the Pacific Coast Sectionals, where she won a bronze medal. She had made it to junior nationals!

Michelle wears a necklace with a little Chinese dragon. This good luck charm was given to her by her grandmother. Michelle has worn it since she was ten years old and never takes it off.

To compete at the national level, a skater must be in top form. Michelle hadn't trained with a coach in nine months. How would she prepare for the biggest competition of her life without a coach at her side?

Michelle didn't know it, but someone had noticed her skating ability and difficult circumstances. Virginia Fratianne, mother of champion skater Linda Fratianne, had seen both Michelle and Karen skate at Ice Castle. When she found out that Michelle didn't have a coach, Virginia asked Linda's former coach, Frank Carroll, to meet with the Kwans. "I was so nervous," recalled Michelle. "I really wanted to impress Frank. I wasn't sure if I belonged with the top skaters Frank coached, but something inside me told me that I might."

After Michelle and Karen had a tryout lesson with Frank, he agreed to coach both girls. Because he was an Ice Castle coach, the sisters became official students and gained access to the entire training center, including the private rink. In addition, they were awarded scholarships that covered many of their expenses. Michelle and Karen's scholarships allowed them to live, train, and go to school at Ice Castle. The facilities included cabins and a dormitory, a dance pavilion, a swimming pool, a Jacuzzi, and a gym. The Kwan sisters couldn't believe their good fortune. "We were living the total skating life," said Michelle.

Even though their expenses were covered and they had a rink in their new backyard, the Kwan family still had to make sacrifices for the sisters. Danny lived in the cabin with Karen and Michelle, but he commuted two hundred miles round-trip, five days a week, for his job with Pacific Bell telephone company in Torrance. The driving and the work made him very tired. Meanwhile Estella and Ron remained in Torrance, where Estella ran the Golden Pheasant. The whole family only saw one another during weekend visits. Michelle missed her mom a lot, but she didn't complain. She knew in her heart that having the chance to follow her skating dream was worth it.

❝I've been lucky enough to pursue my dreams. Center ice is where I love to be. There's no other place more magical.❞

—MICHELLE KWAN

After Michelle and Karen settled into their new home, just three weeks were left before Michelle competed at junior nationals. Would she be ready?

Michelle was worried. She had been more confident in her skating before she began training at the private rink. She said, "I'd won some competitions and thought I knew something about skating. But seeing how hard the top-level skaters worked and how intense they were about what they did showed me how far I had to go." While Michelle focused on landing her jumps without falling, the other skaters worked on smooth, graceful landings. They also paid attention to their overall style, analyzing their hand and leg positions in the connecting moves between jumps. Michelle saw that this careful attention to detail helped the skaters look poised and polished as they performed. Frank knew they had lots of work to do, but he had confidence in his new student. Her love of skating, combined with her skill and dedication, set her apart from other skaters her age.

The pair focused all of their energy on preparing for junior nationals. When Michelle made a mistake in her program during practice, she would stop in frustration. Frank's first job was to teach her how to get up after a fall and keep skating through her program. She certainly couldn't stop in the middle of her program if she made a mistake during the competition! They also worked on the consistency of her jumps. Even though

Michelle had the ability to land triple jumps, she often fell. Frank decided that if she couldn't land a jump 80 percent of the time, it shouldn't be in her program.

Michelle worked hard and learned even more about discipline and dedication in the weeks leading up to the competition. She was so focused that she had dreams about practice. One night Danny overheard Michelle talking to herself in her sleep. She was saying, "It's nothing. It's nothing. It's nothing. . . . " He worried that Michelle was working too hard. In the morning, he pulled his youngest daughter aside, gave her a hug, and told her how proud he was of her hard work. He then told her that he wanted to make sure she was enjoying herself, too. If she wasn't having fun, he didn't want her to keep skating.

❝I dreamed of being the Michael Jordan of my sport. I dreamed of being a legend.**❞**

—MICHELLE KWAN ON HER CHILDHOOD HOPES

Michelle remembered her father's words of advice when she arrived at junior nationals in Florida. She believed that she would do well, but her confidence was rattled after she saw how much older the other skaters looked. There is no minimum or maximum age for each of the skating levels, so junior skaters more than twenty years old would be competing against eleven-year-old Michelle. They were tall and mature and wore makeup. Michelle was definitely one of the youngest skaters at the event. She felt intimidated, and she worried that her plain costume and ponytail made her look immature.

As she prepared for her short program, Michelle reminded herself that she was as good a skater as any in the arena. Just before she took the ice, Frank inspected her up and down but stopped when he got to Michelle's skates. They hadn't been polished in months, and they were covered in scuff marks. Michelle had believed it would be good luck to leave them as they had been when she skated well in regionals and sectionals. Frank, however, knew that the judges at nationals would notice unclean skates. They would not be pleased with her sloppy appearance. He frantically searched for boot polish and put it on her skates as fast as he could. When Michelle took to the ice, her skates were still wet. The last-minute panic had hurt Michelle's concentration, and she had a disastrous performance. She fell on many of her jumps. The following day, her effort in the long program was equally disappointing. A tearful Michelle finished in ninth place.

❝ *Even the disappointments I've had have made me love that slippery ice and the feeling of the wind in my face.* **❞**

—MICHELLE KWAN

When she later thought about her experience at the 1992 junior nationals, Michelle wondered whether Frank had been trying to teach her a lesson in discipline and humility at her first big competition. Skating had always come pretty easily to Michelle, and she was used to winning local competitions. Things were different at the national level. She had to work harder, and getting a medal wasn't guaranteed. Even though the junior nationals were a tough experience for the young skater, Michelle was anxious to prove that she could skate better. She wanted to become a senior lady so she could compete at the 1993 senior nationals and the 1994 Olympics. When she mentioned this plan to Frank, he told her to slow down. He assured her that if she stayed at the junior level for another year and worked hard, she would have a good chance of building her confidence and winning the junior nationals before becoming a senior skater.

Chapter | Four

Practice Makes Perfect

Despite Frank's advice, Michelle wasn't satisfied with skating at the junior level anymore. Karen was also a junior, but she didn't share her sister's impatience to reach the next rank. More than anything else, Michelle wanted to skate with the best, and the best skaters were at the senior level.

Just a couple of months before her twelfth birthday, when Frank was away at a coaching conference, Michelle asked her father to drive her to Los Angeles so she could take the senior test. When Danny asked if Frank had agreed, Michelle mumbled an answer that led her father to believe it was all right with her coach. She ignored Frank's advice and deceived her father for the chance to become a senior.

Michelle passed the test, completing all the required elements—including double and triple jumps and four different spins—with ease. She got her pin and returned home, wondering how she was going to break the news to Frank when he got back. She knew he would be angry. Sure enough, Frank was furious that Michelle had ignored his advice and taken the test behind his back. He was so angry that he didn't talk to her for several days. Frank knew that there was no going back. Once a skater advances to a higher level, she isn't allowed to compete at her previous level. He told Michelle: "You have no idea what it means to be a senior skater. You know next to nothing about the artistic side of skating. You need to understand how to *hear* the music. You are going to have to *transform* your skating."

Although Michelle understood what her coach was saying, she didn't exactly know what he meant. She had to throw herself into training to see the challenges that lay ahead. Michelle's parents wondered whether the pressure was too much for someone so young. But as always, Michelle's love of the sport made her determined to triumph.

❝*I loved the attention I got when I skated, and I was more than happy I'd become a senior skater. It's what I'd wished for my whole life.*❞

—MICHELLE KWAN

She began to study her idols, skaters like Brian Boitano, Peggy Fleming, and Dorothy Hamill, for inspiration. Each of these skaters was great both technically and artistically. While Michelle was able to jump and spin, she knew that her programs lacked the style of a world champion. The individual elements were disjointed. The spins, jumps, and choreography in between didn't flow together as they should. Michelle explained in her autobiography, "In a great program, every movement should flow naturally into the next one. The music and skating should seem like they were meant for each other. The music should seem to *fill* the skater, just like it fills the arena." Michelle and Frank not only had to make her skating smoother, they also had to create two new programs for Michelle that would be suitable for the senior level.

Each skating season, which runs from October through March, a skater needs two programs for competitions. The first is called the short or technical program. It is two and a half minutes long and includes a list of required elements that each skater must complete, in whatever order the skater chooses. The requirements include three jumps, three spins, and two footwork sequences. A mistake on any required element causes the judges to deduct points—or fractions of a point—from a skater's final score. The skater receives one set of marks for technical merit and another for artistic presentation. These scores are then translated into ranks, known as ordinals, and the skater with the most first-place ordinals becomes the leader.

The short program is worth one-third of the overall score.

The rest of the score comes from the long program, also known as the free skate. It is four minutes in length for female skaters and four and a half for the men. In this program, the skaters do not have a list of required elements. However, they do need to include difficult moves to win top technical marks. The technical score reflects the program's difficulty and the skater's technique in the spins, footwork, and jumps. The presentation score reflects the choreography and flow of the program. The skater's speed, posture, and musical interpretation also influence the presentation score.

Frank broke down Michelle's on-ice training into three forty-five-minute daily sessions. She spent at least another hour of off-ice training at the gym, where she stretched and lifted weights. With her intense new schedule, Michelle was no longer able to attend school. But that didn't mean she was free from books and studying. Instead, a tutor came to her cabin every day to give her lessons and homework assignments. Michelle still had to squeeze in time to write papers and take tests, just like other kids her age.

Unlike most other twelve-year-olds, though, Michelle traveled to competitions across the country. A few of her performances were even shown on television! In her first year as a senior skater, Michelle won both senior regionals and sectionals. These wins earned her a spot at the U.S. senior nationals in Phoenix, Arizona. Michelle was thrilled but also nervous. Would her first senior nationals be anything like her first junior nationals?

In 1993 Michelle became the youngest senior skater to compete at the U.S. nationals in twenty years.

Frank and Michelle were determined that she skate at a level that would allow her to compete with the country's top skaters, including Tonya Harding and Nancy Kerrigan. Michelle skated well in the practice sessions in Arizona, even though she was in awe to be on the ice with skaters she admired so much. In her long program, Michelle landed four of her six triples and finished sixth. Nancy Kerrigan won the gold with strong jumps and a mature, graceful style. Michelle was happy with her standing, and she believed she had a chance to make the Olympic team the following year.

After nationals Michelle traveled to Italy for her first over-seas competition. She took part in the Gardena Spring Trophy and met young skaters from many different countries. It was a great experience for Michelle. She discovered that she enjoyed skating in a new setting with other skaters who were beginning their careers.

In the competitions following the U.S. nationals, the almost-teen showed how much she enjoyed her skating. Her upbeat music reflected her bubbly personality and Michelle usually wore a big grin when she skated. Michelle got used to people telling her she was a cute kid. She didn't really mind being called "cute." After all, she wasn't even a teenager and hadn't won any big competition as a senior yet.

❝*It's kind of fun skating with older people. It's fun looking at them and smiling at them. I've never met them before. They've been out there a couple of hundred years. I'm just starting.***❞**

—MICHELLE KWAN, TO A REPORTER AT AGE TWELVE

But that was about to change. When she decided to enter the 1993 Olympic Festival in San Antonio, Texas, she had no idea that the Alamodome would be filled with 25,000 fans. Michelle had never skated in front of such a huge crowd. As she stepped onto the ice, she felt very small. But as she began her performance, she heard cheers coming from all directions. The applause was electrifying, and it gave Michelle the sensation of flying. "It was like a dream," she said. It was also Michelle's first gold medal as a senior skater. All of her hard work had paid off!

Michelle wasn't finished yet. The 1994 Olympics were in sight, and Michelle hadn't forgotten her dream of representing the United States on the Olympic team. Perhaps that was the wish Michelle made when she blew out thirteen candles on her birthday cake on July 7, 1993.

The 1993 Olympic Festival is one of Michelle's all-time favorite skating memories.

Chapter | Five

Taller and Wiser

Michelle's second season as a senior started out with some good news. Karen, who had been a junior the year before, passed her test to advance to the senior level. Even though Karen was making improvements in her skating, only Michelle qualified for the 1994 U.S. senior nationals. Just before Michelle traveled to Detroit, Michigan, for the competition, Karen had a dream that Nancy Kerrigan withdrew from the competition and that Michelle came in second place. Michelle reminded Karen that Nancy was the defending national champion and that it was a very unlikely dream.

Strangely enough, Karen's dream came true. During a practice session the day before the short program, Michelle heard a fan ask for Nancy's autograph. When Nancy disappeared behind a curtain leading to the dressing rooms to meet the fan, she let out a terrible yell. She had been hit in the right knee with a metal baton. The injury was so severe that Nancy had to with-draw from the competition. It was later discovered that Nancy's attacker was a friend of Tonya Harding's husband and that Tonya had been involved as well.

Even before the connection to Tonya was discovered, the media rushed to cover the attack. Reporters and photographers swarmed the rink, and skaters couldn't concentrate on their programs. On the second night of the competition, Michelle worked hard to keep her mind on her long program and landed four triples to finish in second place behind Tonya Harding.

YOUNG AND OLD

The oldest skater at the 1994 nationals was twenty-nine-year-old Elaine Zayak, who had won a national champion-ship the year after Michelle was born! The other top skaters were also in their twenties—Nancy Kerrigan was twenty-four and Tonya Harding was twenty-three. Michelle was just thirteen.

Two Olympic spots were open that year for U.S. skaters. The International Skating Union (ISU) determines how many skaters a country can send to the Olympics based on the results of the previous year's world championships. The higher a country's skaters place in the short program, free skate, and overall, the more they are allowed to send to the world championships and Olympic Games the following year. The maximum number for a country is three skaters. The United States generally sends the top finishers at nationals to compete at these international competitions. With her second-place finish, it looked like Michelle would be going to the Olympics along with Tonya Harding. Michelle was thrilled.

Michelle's excitement quickly changed to confusion. The USFSA ruled that if Nancy recovered, she would represent the United States at the games in Lillehammer, Norway. After all, she was the 1993 national champion and was considered the best female skater in the United States. Nancy was America's best hope for a gold medal in figure skating. Although Michelle felt a little disappointed, she understood the reasoning behind the decision to send Nancy.

Soon after Michelle had gotten it through her head that she wouldn't be competing at the Olympics, rumors surfaced that Tonya might have been involved in the attack on Nancy. If this charge could be proven, Tonya would be disqualified, and Michelle would skate in her place. In the end, the USFSA decided to send Michelle to the Olympics as an alternate. It was an unusual situation, but technically she had still met her child-hood goal of attending the 1994 Olympics!

Michelle remembers how crazy the weeks leading up to the games were. "The reporters heard that [I was going to Norway] and suddenly wanted *me*. Little Michelle Kwan was hot news! They came to Lake Arrowhead and camped out outside Ice Castle. They followed me everywhere. They snuck into the rink, trying to chase me down."

The Kwans and Frank were overwhelmed by all of the attention. They decided to hire sports manager Shep Goldberg, who was also Olympic gymnast Mary Lou Retton's manager, to handle the media. Sports managers make contact with the media, schedule interviews, turn down certain requests, make decisions about endorsements, and handle many of the business details that their clients don't have time for. Shep flew to Lake Arrowhead and accompanied Michelle to the games. Because she wasn't technically a member of the Olympic team, Michelle wasn't allowed to stay in the Olympic village (lodgings for athletes near the arenas where the competitions take place).

Since Nancy had recovered and Tonya wasn't found guilty until after the games, Michelle didn't get to skate at the Olympics. She did, however, get to watch the skating from the stands. The top ladies had very strong performances: Nancy narrowly missed winning the gold to Ukranian skater Oksana Baiul.

The events of early 1994 were enough for an entire year's worth of excitement for Michelle, but her time in the spotlight was just beginning. Nancy declared that she wasn't up to competing at the worlds in March because of the physical and emotional stress she had been through. Tonya wasn't allowed to attend the competition because of evidence that she had known about plans for the attack before it happened.

In her autobiography, Michelle called 1994 "my strangest year."

With Nancy and Tonya out of the picture, Michelle and Nicole Bobek, the fourth-place finisher at the 1994 nationals, became the female representatives for the U.S. team at the 1994 world championships in Chiba, Japan. After Nicole failed to make it past the competition's qualifying round, Michelle became her country's only representative in the ladies' competition. She had a big responsibility on her thirteen-year-old shoulders. Even though she was the youngest American skater ever to compete at worlds and wasn't expected to win a medal, the USFSA did expect her to place in the top ten. A top-ten finish would allow the United States to send two skaters to the world championships the following year. If she finished below tenth place, the United States could send only one skater in 1995.

During the short program, Michelle had trouble with her triple lutz. She was in eleventh place, just one spot away from where she needed to be. "I stayed calm," recalled Michelle. "I told myself to forget about placing and about all those other expectations. The most important thing to remember was *my* expectation for myself, which was to skate my best." It was a good moment for Michelle to learn that she thrived under pressure and loved the feeling of all eyes being on her. In the long program, she landed two triple lutzes and smiled her way through the program. Michelle felt the audience was on her side and when she finished, their cheers proved that she had been right. Her scores moved her up to eighth place. She had done what she needed to do for the United States!

Between the attention she received going to the Olympics as an alternate and being the only female to skate for the United States at the world championships, Michelle had become a famous name in the skating world. She was invited to skate in more exhibitions and competitions. The events gave Michelle additional experience performing in front of a large crowd.

Tom Collins, a former skater and skating show producer of the Tour of World Figure Skating Champions, asked Michelle to join the all-star cast that toured the United States in the summer of 1994. The pace was hectic. They skated seventy-six shows, all in different cities. But Michelle had a great time. Her mother came along, and Michelle was thrilled to have her mom all to herself. When she had free time, Michelle and her mom enjoyed going shopping and spending time together.

In addition to skating and seeing the country, the tour gave Michelle a chance to earn some much-needed money and to spend time with her skating heroes. Brian Boitano, Oksana Baiul, and Nancy Kerrigan were all on the tour, and Michelle soaked up their words of skating advice. The other skaters thought Michelle was sweet and cute, a word Michelle grew to dislike because she heard it so much. As much as Michelle enjoyed getting to know the older skaters, she sometimes wished someone else on the tour was close to her age. In the end, Michelle's closest friend on the tour became Harris Collins, Tom's brother. Even though he was more than thirty years older than Michelle, he shared her wacky, teenage sense of humor. On the bus between cities, the two would tell each other jokes and silly stories while the rest of the skaters tried to sleep.

Michelle turned fourteen that summer. She had grown three inches and had gained twenty pounds since 1992. She was five feet two inches tall and just under one hundred pounds. Her new body took some getting used to. Although Michelle wasn't as light as she had been, she had more strength and power in her skating. She felt that she could put more weight into the edges of her blades, which helped the technical side of her skating. She couldn't wait to see how the 1994–1995 skating season would unfold.

Michelle donates all the stuffed animals given to her by fans to a local children's hospital in Los Angeles.

Frank and Michelle had hired a choreographer named Lori Nichol to put together new routines for Michelle. They chose Lori after noticing that she was especially skilled in designing programs that showed off a skater's strengths. Before putting the whole program together, they needed to select unique music and to choose moves that would catch the judges' attention. Michelle explained the process of creating her programs in one of her books: "We discuss where to put the jumps and think about footwork and spins and spirals. It's a long process. Sometimes we'll spend one hour deciding what I'll do for about two seconds of the program!"

After a couple of weeks working with Lori and Frank, Michelle had two challenging new routines. Her difficult long program included seven triple jumps, more than any other female skater. Much to her surprise, Michelle was considered the favorite to win the 1995 nationals. Her old rivals Nancy and

Tonya were gone from amateur competition. Nancy had turned professional. Over the summer, the USFSA had taken away Tonya's U.S. nationals gold medal and had banned her from skating in USFSA events, including nationals, for the rest of her life. Michelle took these changes in stride. "It'd be great to be the next national champion. I don't think there's any pressure, though. I'm still the underdog," she said.

She may have been the underdog, but Michelle knew that her skating was improving. As she traveled to Providence, Rhode Island, for the nationals, she couldn't help but wonder if this was her year to win gold. In the short program, Michelle wobbled on a triple lutz–double toe loop combination and found herself in third place behind Tonia Kwiatkowski and Nicole Bobek. In the long program, Michelle started off well, completing her first five elements flawlessly. She seemed to lose her concentration, however, when she skipped a jump combination (two jumps in a row) and had to quickly improvise part of her program. She later fell on a triple lutz. Afterward she said, "I was just a little off and a little slow." Nicole Bobek, who had a reputation for being talented but inconsistent, won the gold with a mature, sophisticated program. She skated with good speed and high jumps and had a strong presence on the ice. Michelle finished just behind her, and the two of them began preparing for the 1995 worlds in Birmingham, England.

Michelle felt confident in her skating and in her programs at worlds. In the short program, she skated well but found herself in fifth place. One critic said that while she had turned in a smooth performance, "her jumps still lack height and her skating still lacks speed." In the long program, Michelle was determined to move up in the standings. She landed each jump cleanly and even added a double toe loop to a triple lutz to make it a combination jump at the end of the program. She skated with such skill and enthusiasm that she received the only standing ovation of the entire ladies' competition. After finishing her routine, Michelle broke down in tears. She knew she had never skated better in her life. She told a reporter, "It was so overwhelming with all the American flags waving and everybody standing. It was just incredible."

The other women also skated well, though none of them had seven triples in their programs. But what they lacked in jumps, they more than made up for in style. Despite the fact that Michelle was the only skater to skate two clean programs with no bobbles or falls, she came in fourth place, behind Lu Chen of China, Surya Bonaly of France, and Nicole Bobek.

A frustrated Michelle wondered why she hadn't placed higher. The biggest difference between herself and the other skaters was that they were older and looked more like women. Michelle wore her hair in a ponytail and still didn't wear makeup.

Michelle and Frank decided that it was time for Michelle to change her look and become more grown-up. That meant makeup and a new hairstyle. She hoped her new look would give her more confidence on the ice and get the judges' attention, proving to them that she was a seasoned skater and not just a cute kid.

---

66 *Not only is she the star of today, she's the star of tomorrow.* 99

—SHEP GOLDBERG, MICHELLE'S MANAGER

Her appearance wasn't all Michelle wanted to change. She wanted to become a more artistic skater, even though she knew this wouldn't be an easy task. She explained: "There's a lot of tension between [artistry and athleticism in skating]. On the one hand, you need incredible precision and athleticism for the jumps and other technical parts of your program. On the other, you want to find an open, flowing way to express what the music and skating mean to you. These are two very different states of mind. Blending them together is what makes figure skating such an unusual and difficult sport."

Frank, Lori, and Michelle were faced with the task of creating more mature, dramatic programs. They found just the right inspiration for her long program with the music of *Salome,* by

German composer Richard Strauss. The piece is an interpretation of the biblical story of Salome. Salome performs the dance of the seven veils for King Herod Antipas in return for the head of John the Baptist. The dramatic music appealed to Michelle, and she loved the idea of playing a role while she skated.

As Salome, Michelle wore a beautiful two-piece violet-and-gold costume and bright red lipstick and piled her hair high on her head. When the fifteen-year-old took the ice at the Skate America competition in October 1995, her first public performance of the new routine, few people even recognized her. Critics weren't sure what to think of her new look. Some said that she was trying to grow up too fast, and they missed the sweet innocence of her earlier programs. "Her youth seemed unnecessarily lost," wrote a reporter for the *New York Times*. When asked about the new style in interviews, Michelle said, "It's good to have another look. It's very different for me." Not only was her look transformed, Michelle was skating with a new confidence. She won the competition, beating reigning world champion Lu Chen and American rival Nicole Bobek by landing seven triple jumps in the long program. The new style had paid off. Would it also allow Michelle to become the national or world champion?

Chapter Six

The Best in the World

Skating as Salome did more than just give Michelle confidence—it made her feel like she belonged. As she traveled from competition to competition that year, she was no longer a ponytailed little girl. She finally felt like she fit in as a senior skater. For the first time, Michelle believed that if she skated her best, she could win any competition.

66 *Frank [Carroll] understands very deeply what is needed to become a champion in figure skating. That [it's] more than just teaching skating. He understands musicality, costuming . . . what his skaters must do to satisfy the judges.* 99

—JOHN NICKS, AMERICAN FIGURE SKATING COACH

Michelle kept this in mind as she began her short program at the 1996 nationals in San Jose, California. It was an exciting night for Michelle—Karen was there competing as well. Skating to flamenco music, Michelle cleanly completed every element and showed off her polished, refined new style for the judges. Entering the free skate in first place, she soared through her program, landing each jump and skating like she already had the gold. No other skater could match her difficult and sophisticated performance, and all nine judges gave her first-place marks. Tonia Kwiatkowski finished in second and Tara Lipinski in third. Nicole Bobek, the defending champion, had to drop out of the competition due to an injury.

> Michelle and Karen both skated at the 1996 national championships, making them the first sisters to do so in thirty-six years.

Michelle was finally national champion, but almost as exciting was Karen's fifth-place finish. Over the years, while Karen had continued to train with Michelle, she had also developed other interests. She had decided that she wanted to go to college, so Michelle knew this might be the last time they skated together. Karen's strong finish made the night even more special for Michelle. Danny and Estella couldn't have been prouder of their daughters.

Having stood atop the winner's podium at nationals, Michelle was determined to be there again at worlds. But she faced stiff competition from Lu Chen and Japan's Midori Ito, another former world champion. They were both older and had much more experience in international competitions. Still, Michelle felt in her heart that if she skated her best, she would be unbeatable. Her short program opened with an unusual spiral sequence before getting into the jumps, which included a triple lutz, double toe loop combination, and double axel. Her performance was called "elegant" and "impeccable." The pressure was on, but Michelle was sure she could deliver with her Salome routine and her seven triple jumps, including a triple toe–triple toe combination and two triple lutzes.

> Michelle has a little teddy bear backpack that she takes with her to each competition. Frank liked to make the bear perform perfect triple lutzes while Michelle warmed up.

As she waited backstage to skate her long program, Michelle was in first place. But then came the thunderous applause and word that Lu Chen had received two perfect 6.0s for presentation. No woman had ever received a perfect mark at worlds. For a moment, Michelle panicked. How could she beat that? Then she realized that not all of Lu's marks were perfect. She had a few 5.8s, so if Michelle could receive 6.0s and 5.9s, she could edge by her and hold on to first place. Her head was spinning: "I thought I would have to do a quadruple loop [a jump no female skater has ever landed] to win. I brought myself back to earth again and said, 'Heck, I'll go for everything. Why not?'"

Michelle began cautiously but gained confidence as she landed jump after jump. She was skating perfectly as she neared the end of her routine. She had just one jump left, a double axel, but she suddenly realized that if she performed a triple jump instead, she would have one more triple than Lu. At the last moment, Michelle turned her double axel into a triple toe loop. She kept her body straight in the air and pulled out a perfect landing. She'd done it! Before the program had even ended, the American flags started to wave triumphantly in the stands.

Michelle shed happy tears as she left the ice and awaited her scores with Frank in the kiss-and-cry area. She received two 6.0s along with a lot of 5.9s. When the scores were tallied, most judges placed her ahead of Lu. She was the new ladies world champion! It seemed that overnight, Michelle had gone from skating with the best in the world to being the best. Those who had been unsure what to think of her new look began praising it. The *New York Times* reporter who had criticized her after the Skate America competition wrote, "In recent months, Kwan has grown into the part, not only with cosmetic changes, but with her ripened skating style—the elegant hand movement, the stroking, the clean edges that allow her to glide over the ice in what her coach calls a graceful 'ooze.'"

After she won her first worlds, Michelle slept with her medal.

Following worlds, requests for interviews and television appearances came pouring in. Michelle was glad she had hired Shep to help her through everything. He told her that when she spoke with reporters, she should be herself and answer questions truthfully. Michelle was even invited to the White House to meet President Bill Clinton, but she was just too busy to squeeze it into her schedule. Michelle couldn't believe she was turning down the president!

Even though she had become a celebrity, Michelle still had two more years of high school to complete. In between practices and appearances, she studied as much as she could. She was determined not to let her grades slip because she knew that all of her skating success wouldn't last forever. She wanted to go to college someday, possibly Harvard, and become a lawyer.

But it was hard to think too much about college when she had fan mail to answer and television appearances to make. Michelle was so busy that she hardly had time to stop and enjoy it all. This was what she had wanted since she was seven years old, but her life still felt surreal. "It's not that I felt different," Michelle explained. "But I definitely was in a different place with a new outlook."

❝*I love to travel. Part of the excitement of a competition is getting to go to a place I've never been before. My parents and I always try to take little side trips when we're in a new country.*❞

—MICHELLE KWAN

Her family and her old friends at Ice Castle and on the summer skating tour kept Michelle grounded. They treated her the same way they always had. Michelle had become good friends with Brian Boitano, Canadian skater Elvis Stojko, and American pairs skaters Jeni Meno and Todd Sand. Michelle was still the youngest, but her national and world championship wins made her feel more like she fit in with the others, many of whom were also world and national champions. And of course, time on tour meant more time joking around with Harris. Apart from her sister, Harris had become her best friend.

---

66 *Skating is in my heart, not my head.* 99

—MICHELLE KWAN

Skating on tour was also a nice break from the pressures of competition. There were no medals to win or lose, just enthusiastic crowds to entertain. The arenas were always dark except for the spotlight on the skater, so Michelle sometimes forgot the audience was right in front of her until she heard their applause. As usual, she loved connecting with them in each city, night after night.

Chapter | Seven

A Hard Landing

Even though being on tour was supposed to be a fun break from the competitive skating season, Michelle couldn't help but wonder what 1997 had in store for her. She was the reigning national and world champion, and she knew that the titles were hers to lose. She felt more pressure than ever. She needed new objectives and goals for her skating.

These thoughts were pushed into the back of Michelle's mind after June 1, 1996, the day Harris Collins died. The tour was in Chicago, Illinois, and Harris had just told the skaters that they had only five minutes until showtime. Suddenly Michelle heard screams. Harris had fallen, and he was going to the hospital, but no one knew what had happened. It was time to start the show. Michelle had tears of sadness and confusion streaming down her face when she was announced. As the show went on and no word of Harris came to the arena, Michelle figured that he must be okay. It wasn't until after the show that Michelle learned that her forty-nine-year-old friend had died of a heart attack. Michelle was devastated. She had known a few people who had died, but they were all very old. And she had never lost a good friend.

The tour continued from city to city, and little by little it got easier for Michelle to perform. The fans helped her a lot. She said, "Every night when the announcer introduced me and I skated out onto the ice, I heard the warm, wonderful sound from the audience. It made me forget everything . . . except that I wanted to skate for them."

When the tour was over in July, Michelle returned to Lake Arrowhead and her parents' new home. Danny and Estella had managed to buy a home of their own near Ice Castle. Even though Michelle didn't skate as a professional, she still won large cash awards (up to $50,000 for first place in amateur competitions), and she was able to take endorsement deals that earned her even more money. Her skating expenses were all covered by her income and there was more left over than the Kwans had ever imagined. Most of this money was Michelle's, but she was as generous with her parents as they had been with her for so many years with their many sacrifices. Even though the house wasn't large, it seemed big to Michelle, who was used to her small cabin at Ice Castle. The house also seemed empty. Ron had been in college for a couple of years already, and it was Karen's freshman year at Boston University. Michelle missed sharing everything with her big sister. Fortunately, Karen was just a phone call away, and Michelle's parents were also great listeners.

When she's not on the ice, Michelle likes to Rollerblade, read, chat online with friends, shop, cook, and watch movies. Her favorite movies include *Gladiator, Titanic, The Cutting Edge, Jerry Maguire,* and *Braveheart.*

Michelle turned sixteen that summer. In addition to the pressures she had on the ice, she also had to deal with the regular pressures of being a teenager. Just after her birthday, Michelle took her driving test. She had never been as nervous at a competition as she was behind the wheel with her examiner in the car, grading her every move. "My hands were literally shaking on the wheel," Michelle confessed. "I can stand in front of a panel of judges without the slightest knee wobble, but this one examiner threw me into a panic." Michelle failed her first test but passed the exam a few weeks later. With some of the money she had saved up from competitions and tours, she bought her very own car!

Michelle had become used to dealing with the media, having her face on magazine covers, and having disagreements with Frank now and then. Even though Michelle respected her coach and valued his opinion about her skating, the two didn't always see eye to eye. The pair usually had one or two big fights each year, and when these disagreements happened, Michelle turned to her family for advice. Danny and Estella were always there to offer their support and understanding, which was exactly what Michelle needed in her life.

Before the 1996–1997 skating season began, Michelle asked her father for advice for the coming year. She knew she would have some things to work on. Her father told her that she needed to appreciate everything she had and to remember to have perspective on skating. Even though it was important, it wasn't her whole life.

66*She loved the sport until she was about fifteen. But then it became the podium and winning that she loved.*99

—DANNY KWAN

As the 1996–1997 skating season began, Michelle felt like she was off-kilter. She had trouble incorporating her dad's words of advice into her life. She missed Karen and Harris. She had new, polished routines, and she was the one to beat at competitions. Still, she didn't have any skating goals for herself, like she usually did. Instead of skating for the joy of it, she had become preoccupied with not losing her titles. "I couldn't see the next challenge," Michelle later admitted. "I could only see how far down I had to fall. Instead of reaching higher, I tried to grip my position more tightly. I tried to hold on with all my might. *Just don't fall,* I said to myself. *Work harder. Don't fall.*"

Michelle started the season well, winning the first two competitions of the season. But unlike the previous season, when she had felt on top of the world and unbeatable, she started doubting herself on the ice. No matter what she did, she kept picturing herself falling. When asked about the pressure of being a defending national champion and gold medal favorite, Michelle told reporters she was dealing with it by just remembering it was a sport and by having fun. But she couldn't shake the image of falling on the ice.

In a practice session at nationals the day before the short program, Michelle fell again and again. She fell five times while attempting her triple lutz. On the day of the performance, Michelle was randomly selected to be the second skater, out of twenty, in the short program. Many fans hadn't even arrived at the stadium when she took the ice. In her performance, she played the role of Desdemona, a character from Shakespeare's play *Othello*. A quiet crowd watched as

Michelle fought to hold on to the landings of her triple lutz–double toe combination and her double axel. Although it wasn't one of her strongest performances, it was still enough to put her in first place. In second was a young jumping sensation named Tara Lipinski.

In the long program, Michelle's first combination, a triple lutz–double toe, went well. In her next combination, she slid off her edge on the landing of the second jump and sprawled across the ice. Later in the program, she put her hand on the ice to avoid falling out of her triple flip. Each fall or hand down meant another deduction in her technical marks. Then on her next triple jump, Michelle fell again. Even though she was skating poorly, the crowd rallied behind her, and their cheers helped her skate the rest of her routine without any mistakes. But the damage had been done. Afterward Michelle didn't know how to describe what had happened. "I was a little shocked," she told reporters. "I was standing up and then I was on the ice. I panicked and . . . got a little off balance."

She watched with dismay as second-place Tara executed seven perfect triple jumps to take the evening's top marks. Tara was just beginning her second year as a senior skater, but she was already known for her incredible jumps and consistency. At fourteen years old, she became the youngest-ever U.S. figure skating national champion. Michelle finished in second.

Michelle didn't have much time to shake off her loss before
the world championships. Fortunately, she had a great support
system. The first skater to call and talk to Michelle was Brian
Boitano. He told her to get rid of her negative thoughts and visu-
alize herself skating a clean program. Rather than thinking
about what could go wrong, she had to think about doing it
right. Michelle knew she needed to take Brian's advice. She also
had to remember what Frank and her father had told her about
enjoying her skating.

Even with her new mind-set, it was hard not to listen to
what reporters said about her at the 1997 world championships
in Lausanne, Switzerland. They predicted that the event would
be a matchup between young Tara's strong technical skating
and Michelle's artistry. It was ironic for Michelle, who had been
known as a technician prior to her turn as Salome. But she was
now seen as the more seasoned, artistic skater.

Michelle tried to shut out the predictions and voices in her head—especially the one that had been telling her she was going to fall—as she prepared for her short program. She stumbled out of the triple lutz in her triple lutz–double toe combination jump and was fourth heading into the free skate. Michelle was frustrated and disappointed with herself.

❝I don't know if it's a changing of my body. I try to adjust as well as I can. It's been a little difficult the whole year. I've got to get my head straight and be more aggressive.❞

—MICHELLE KWAN, AT 1997 WORLDS

Then two things happened that helped Michelle get her priorities back in order. Legendary coach Carlo Fassi suddenly passed away in Lausanne. He had coached Peggy Fleming and Dorothy Hamill. Although Michelle didn't know Carlo very well, she had seen him training fellow skater Nicole Bobek each day at Ice Castle. The skating community was saddened by the loss and was amazed that Nicole managed to skate at worlds despite her grief. At the same time, Michelle heard that Olympic champion Scott Hamilton had been diagnosed with cancer. Suddenly her long program didn't seem quite so important.

When Michelle took the ice for her long program, she knew

she wasn't going to fall. She felt the familiar rush she got when she was in the groove and enjoying skating her routine.

❝ *I've learned that focusing on what I need to do works much better than thinking about what I shouldn't do. It keeps me positive.* **❞**

—MICHELLE KWAN

She made one small mistake when she turned a triple jump into a double, but she still ended up winning the long program. One skating critic wrote that Michelle had "regained her poise . . . demonstrating her unmatched balance of artistry and athleticism." In the final standings, Michelle still came in second behind Tara, but she knew that her streak of negative thoughts and skating struggles was behind her. As she accepted her silver medal, she felt happier than she had in a long time.

Chapter | Eight

Chasing the Gold

Michelle was definitely in the right mind-set as she started preparing for her Olympic year. As soon as 1997 worlds was over, Lori, Frank, and Michelle got to work on her all-important new routines.

That summer while Michelle was on tour again, she listened to the music that she and Lori had selected for her free skate. The piece was from *Lyra Angelica,* by William Alwyn. Although Michelle hadn't been sure if the music was right for her the first time she heard it, it soon haunted her. "Music is the most important element in skating—it inspires every jump, every stroke of the blade, every tilt of the head. It tells me what to do and how to feel," she said. "I really have to love our musical selections because between competitions and daily practices, I'll listen to them thousands of times during the year." Lori and Frank had a feeling that the music was perfect for Michelle.

In 1993, at her very first U.S. national championships, Michelle finished in sixth place.

By her third year as a senior skater, Michelle had already gained many fans. They admired her amazing jumping abilities as well as her youthful enthusiasm.

Michelle surprised the skating world with the mature, emotional style of her "Salome" program. Here she performs at the 1996 world championships, where she won the gold.

Michelle and her older sister, Karen *(left)*, were inseparable on and off the ice. They spent long hours at the rink with coach Frank Carroll *(center)*.

During the 1996–1997 skating season, Michelle struggled with her jumps and her confidence. Here she falls during her "Taj Mahal" free skate at the 1997 U.S. nationals.

Michelle has worn this lucky necklace, given to her by her grandmother, since she was ten years old.

At the 1998 Olympic Games, Michelle skated her long program to *Lyra Angelica*. Although she finished with a silver medal, fans around the world admired her for her grace and composure in defeat.

In her short program at the 2002 U.S. nationals, Michelle shows off her trademark spiral as she skates to music by Rachmaninoff.

"Fields of Gold" was one of Michelle's exhibition pieces in 2002 and 2003. Here she performs a spread eagle.

Michelle cherished her eighth trip to the top step of the national championship podium in January 2004.

"Frank and I had seen that peaceful quality of hers in practice. We just hadn't given her a vehicle to express it," said Lori. Michelle said the music reminded her of angels and clouds and being free.

One of Michelle's favorite off-ice activities is fishing. During an Alaskan fishing trip when she was on her summer tour, she went fishing with fellow skaters Todd Eldredge and Lloyd Eisler and caught a twenty-five-pound salmon!

By the time Michelle returned to Ice Castle from touring, she was more than ready to get back to work. She had a beautiful new program to skate and her Olympic dream to focus on. Michelle had so much renewed enthusiasm when she skated onto the ice each day that she didn't even feel the pain in her left boot—that is, until she dug into her toe pick to push off for a triple toe loop in practice one day. What had at first seemed like a problem with her skate was definitely something wrong with her toe. In August she was diagnosed with a stress fracture in her second toe, meaning that the bone had weakened but wasn't broken. Michelle's doctor told her that she had most likely had the injury for nearly a year. He advised her to take care of her foot or it could turn into a bad break.

Michelle was determined that her toe wouldn't slow her down. She completely forgot about the pain when she skated her short program, which was to a piano concerto by Russian composer Sergey Rachmaninoff, and her free skate to *Lyra Angelica.*

Michelle was skating with renewed happiness that she claimed had come from her struggles of the year before. She had a new perspective on the previous season, saying, "I'm glad last year happened. Everything had happened so fast, I didn't appreciate what I had already done. I didn't enjoy it. I was so worried about winning, it was as if I was caught up in my own web. I kept asking myself, why am I here if I don't love it? Why am I torturing myself? It's supposed to be fun, and I thought I'd die if I didn't win."

One of Michelle's pastimes is copying inspirational quotes and pieces of poetry into her diary. One of her favorite passages is from the book *Walden,* written by Henry David Thoreau: "However mean your life is, meet it and live it; do not shun it and call it hard names. It is not so bad as you are. It looks poorest when you are richest. The fault-finder will find faults even in paradise."

In October, Michelle took her new attitude and outlook with her to her first competition of the season, Skate America, in Detroit, Michigan. She was excited to show off her new long program. She had helped choose a beautiful sky blue costume that reminded her of what she saw when she heard the music. She wasn't skating as a character, like Salome or Desdemona. Instead she was simply herself, a skater performing to beautiful music.

The media were wondering if the old Michelle was back, and the crowds gathered in Detroit were anxious to see Michelle warm up before the competition. She fell on a double axel and the crowd gasped, but she wasn't rattled. It was just a warm-up, her chance to get a feel for the ice. When she skated her routines, she made no mistakes. Michelle took home the gold medal.

A week later, Michelle was in Halifax, Nova Scotia, for Skate Canada. Frank had been unable to accompany her, so for the first time ever, Michelle was alone backstage. Her toe had been bothering her that week, and she had nearly withdrawn from the competition. But she wanted to skate her new programs as many times as she could before the Olympics. All was going well until she attempted her triple toe jump at the end of her long program. Suddenly the throbbing pain was back, and in her last move, a simple butterfly jump, in which a skater's body stays horizontal to the ice while her legs twirl behind her, she crashed to the ice.

Even though she still managed to win the competition, Michelle feared that she had really injured her toe this time. She was right. Her doctor ordered her off the ice, and Michelle's foot was put in a cast. She was forced to withdraw from competitions for the rest of 1997. But Michelle knew she had to be back in time for nationals in January 1998. It was her Olympic year, and she needed to be ready.

Michelle was more than ready when she returned to the ice at nationals and made history with her fifteen perfect 6.0s. "She found something out about herself in Philadelphia," Lori Nichol said. "She learned she could feel serenity and joy on the ice, in front of a crowd, in an incredibly pressurized moment. And she did it after having been off the ice almost a month from her injury. She knows now that she can deal with anything, good or bad. She's saying, 'I was good—now how much better can I be?'"

When she was a little girl, Michelle made three wishes: to go to the Olympics and skate for the United States, to skate well there, and to win the gold medal.

Michelle wanted to find out just how much better she could be when she traveled to Nagano, Japan, for the Olympic Games.

The women's skating team was the strongest anyone could ever remember, and hopes abounded that they would sweep the medals. Michelle was the favorite for gold, and teammates Tara Lipinski and Nicole Bobek were expected to win silver and bronze. Even though the media talked endlessly about whether Michelle would win the gold, she tried not to focus on medals. Instead of marching in the opening ceremonies or staying with the other athletes in the Olympic village, Michelle arrived at the games later and stayed with her family at a hotel a few miles away. Frank had been concerned that the noise and commotion in the Olympic village would be distracting. Michelle hoped that by isolating herself, she would have fewer reporters and disturbances to worry about.

When Michelle glided onto the ice to skate her short program, she saw the five intertwined Olympic rings and almost had to pinch herself. She was really there—skating at the Olympics! "Just think," Frank said to her. "You've always wanted to do this. And here you are." Michelle didn't make a single mistake in her short program and was in first place heading to the long program, which was scheduled two days later.

In the meantime, Michelle tried to stay calm by talking to her sister on the phone and e-mailing friends back home. She had her practice sessions to keep her occupied. After her morning practice on the day of her long skate, Michelle tried to take a nap in her hotel room. She tossed and turned for four hours before deciding that she was too wound up. Her mind racing, Michelle arrived at the rink early.

The arena was packed with spectators and other Olympians who had come to see who would win the gold medal. Michelle was the first skater in the last group scheduled to skate that evening. The last group contained the top six skaters after the short program—the skaters who had a chance to win the medals. Some skaters don't like to go first. Judges often give the first skater lower marks in case another skater in the group has a better performance. But just a few nights before, Russian singles skater Ilia Kulik had won the gold medal in the men's skating competition, and he had also been first in the final group.

As the first strains of *Lyra Angelica* filled the air, Michelle reminded herself to have fun. She focused all of her energy on avoiding errors. She completed all her jumps, but some of the landings looked tentative. She seemed cautious, and her performance didn't feel as open and free as it had at nationals. At the end, she saw American flags waving and felt relief wash over her. She had done it. She had skated a clean program. Michelle let the tears flow as she skated over to Frank in the kiss-and-cry area to await her scores. She received 5.7s and 5.8s for technical merit and all 5.9s for presentation. Michelle was happy, even though she knew that the judges had left room for someone to pass her.

That someone was Tara Lipinski. Despite winning lots of competitions in the 1996–1997 season, Tara hadn't been skating her best in the 1997–1998 season, and she had placed behind Michelle all year. But she gave the performance of her young life in the long program at the Olympics. She skated with energy and enthusiasm and landed every jump perfectly. Her program contained a triple loop–triple loop combination and included a heart-stopping triple toe–half loop–triple salchow combination in the final seconds of her music. Her program had a higher degree of difficulty than Michelle's, so even though Michelle won higher artistic marks, Tara's technical marks put her ahead of everybody. She became the youngest figure skater to win the gold in Olympic history.

Although Michelle felt like she had let the gold medal slip through her fingers, she tried to stay positive. She had won a silver medal at the Olympics, and two of her three dreams had come true. She even got to hear the American national anthem played over the loudspeaker that night.

After the medal ceremony was over, Michelle called Karen, and the two sisters cried tears of happiness as well as disappointment. "It was the hardest moment of my life," Michelle admitted. "I was so close to what I'd always dreamed of that I could taste it. Afterwards, I just tried to hold it together." She knew she hadn't skated with the abandon she had at nationals. "She was a bit conservative," Frank said. "She was going for accuracy and consistency. Her performance was very held in. It was not the feeling of flying."

Even though Michelle's Olympic medal may not have been the color it was in her dreams, hers was a huge story in skating. Despite the fact that Tara was the Olympic winner, Michelle received more endorsement offers and magazine cover stories. Even though she wasn't the Olympic champion, she was the people's champion. Her sportsmanship embodied the spirit of the games, and the world loved her for smiling through her tears as she placed second.

❝ *What is a champion? To me, a champion isn't someone who never loses or falls down. It's someone who gets back up. Someone who has heart.* ❞

—MICHELLE KWAN

In 1997 Michelle had released her autobiography, *Heart of a Champion,* and after the Olympics she added another chapter. Disney signed her on to make television skating specials as well as to write motivational books for teens and preteens. With

Shep's guidance, Michelle accepted offers to endorse a variety of products, including cars, yogurt, and soap. She made it a point not to endorse any product she wouldn't use herself. But even with the restrictions she placed on the products she endorsed, Michelle was making over a million dollars a year. The money gave her and her family financial freedom.

Michelle took acting classes in Los Angeles and was a guest star on the television show *Sabrina, the Teenage Witch.*

Tara turned professional just weeks after the Olympic Games and started skating with Stars on Ice, another tour featuring past champions. She told reporters that her decision was based on two factors—first, she had fulfilled her dream of being an Olympic champion, and second, she wanted to spend more time with her family, who had been living apart during her amateur skating career. She and Michelle will never again compete with each other in an amateur competition.

A month after the Olympics, Michelle won the world championships. It was clear that she was the fans' favorite by the way the crowd cheered before and after her programs. People were impressed with the way she had handled herself with grace and dignity after the Olympics. "Even now parents come up to me and say, 'The way you handled your loss in Nagano made you a great role model for my kids,'" Michelle said. "But it wasn't anything I had to work on. I mean, I didn't hide anything. I was upset I didn't win; I was crying afterward. But what are you going to do, hit the wall about it? I was lucky enough to have parents who taught me about sportsmanship." She admitted that it wasn't always easy to smile for all the reporters who asked her how it felt to lose. But Michelle had new dreams she wanted to fulfill. It was time to move on.

Chapter Nine

School Days

Michelle had more than just skating dreams. She was seventeen and about to graduate from high school. One of her biggest goals was to go to college. With her grade point average a high 3.61 (out of a possible 4.0), Michelle had her choice of colleges to attend. She had always imagined going to school in Boston, near Karen. She was accepted at Harvard University, which is close to Boston University, her sister's school. As the time to choose a school loomed closer, however, Michelle decided to stay closer to home, her parents, Frank, and Ice Castle. After all, she wasn't planning to give up skating while she went to college. She wanted to try to do both—eventually.

Before starting college, Michelle decided to take one year off to enjoy herself and keep skating. One of the first things she had scheduled was a family vacation, the entire Kwan family's first together in a long time. They traveled to Hawaii, where

Michelle mixed sunbathing with snorkeling and scuba diving.

When she returned home, a new season was on the horizon. Michelle wanted to prove to herself that she was still at the

Because of her academic success, Michelle received the 1997 Dial Award, given to the top graduating athlete in the country.

top of her sport despite her Olympic loss. Just as she had done three years earlier, eighteen-year-old Michelle got a new look. She had always had long hair, but she cut it into a short "boy cut" before the start of the 1998–1999 skating season. The new hairdo was a nice change for Michelle.

The season got off to a good start. She won the Goodwill Games and the World Professional Championships, which was opened to amateurs in 1998. The 1999 national championships were held in January at the Delta Center in Salt Lake City, Utah, the home of the 2002 Winter Olympic Games. Michelle knew a win there would feel extra special and might mean good things for her in 2002. Michelle's biggest competition was from two thirteen-year-old girls, Naomi Nari Nam and Sarah Hughes, who had just become senior ladies. Michelle was clearly a more seasoned skater. She earned a 6.0 on her short program, which she skated to the music of *Carmen*. Even though she fell on a triple lutz in her long program, she easily won nationals. The rest of her program was flawless and she nailed her other six triple jumps, including a triple-triple. "It was one of those performances where I just let it go," Michelle said. She earned ten 5.9s and eight 5.8s for her efforts.

Michelle is the only figure skater with her own interactive video game, *Michelle Kwan Figure Skating*.

At her next event, the world championships, held in Helsinki, Finland, the competition was much more fierce, and Michelle had a cold. Unlike most of her previous appearances at worlds, Michelle had to first skate in a qualifying round. A change in rules dictated that a skater had to skate a qualifying round, then a short program, and then a free skate. The reasoning behind this new, more difficult schedule was that it would weed out lesser skaters so that only the best would be able to skate in the remaining short and long programs. The inclusion of the qualifying round also changed the scoring system. The qualifying skate is worth 20 percent of the total score, the short program 30 percent, and the long program 50 percent. But for Michelle, one of the top skaters in the world, the change only served to wear her down even more. She fell on a double axel and skidded across the ice during her short program. "I wasn't on," Michelle admitted. "I haven't been on all week. Usually I am pretty solid and consistent, but I've been a little shaky."

She was still feeling under the weather during her free skate, and she was sluggish. Although she didn't fall, she stepped out of a triple lutz and turned a double axel into a single. She landed six triple jumps, but it wasn't good enough. She lost the gold to the Russian Maria Butyrskaya, who landed seven triples. Michelle may have been disappointed with her second-place finish, but she had other things to occupy her mind, namely getting ready for college.

Michelle enrolled at the University of California at Los Angeles (UCLA) in the fall of 1999. She decided that she wanted the complete college experience. She was planning to live in the dormitories, go to parties, and make friends her own age. After having been tutored since she was thirteen, Michelle was excited to hang out with people her own age who weren't skaters. She spent her first semester eating pizza and going to football games as well as studying, attending classes, and training at a nearby rink. It was hard to fit it all in, but Michelle loved her jam-packed schedule.

> ❝ *Ever since seventh or eighth grade, I've had private tutors and never really had the chance to meet other students. I decided to go all out with college, stay in the dorms, meet other people. I just want to be a normal student. . . . I want the whole experience I missed out on in high school.* ❞
>
> —MICHELLE KWAN

When the skating season began in October, Michelle was ready. She was especially excited about her two new programs. The music for her short program was an instrumental version of "A Day in the Life," by the Beatles, one of her favorite bands. The jazzy music was a departure for Michelle from her typically classical selections, but it seemed to suit her. Her long program contained musical selections from *The Red Violin* movie sound track. "There's something very compelling about this music," Michelle said. Unfortunately, judges and audiences weren't as drawn to it as Michelle was. The piece was somber and perhaps too contemplative to be attention-getting.

Despite the music, Michelle won her first two competitions at Skate America and Skate Canada. Even though she was off to a good start, Michelle's skating wasn't on the level it had been just a couple of years before. This may have been because her competition was suddenly adding more difficult jumps and combinations. Jere Longman of the *New York Times* wrote: "The technical aspect of her skating has remained static while her opponents have upped the ante with dazzling triple jumps." Frank thought she needed to spend more time on the ice and less time in the dorm. But Michelle wanted to complete some more of the season before making any decisions about the future.

As the 1999–2000 season continued, it became obvious to Michelle that Frank was right. First she lost the Grand Prix finals in Lyon, France, to Russia's Irina Slutskaya. Irina and other skaters at the competition had difficult triple-triple jump combinations in their programs, while Michelle had only triple-double combinations. Michelle's technical scores couldn't match those of the skaters with the harder jumps. A few weeks after the Grand Prix finals, Michelle fell on a triple toe loop during her short program at nationals. She was embarrassed to have fallen on such an easy jump—she hadn't missed it in a competition in four years! Even though she rallied to win the event, edging out competitors Sarah Hughes and another up-and-comer, Sasha Cohen, Michelle decided that she needed to make some changes in her life.

That spring she moved out of the dorms and bought a house near the training center in El Segundo. "Living on campus, it was hard to concentrate on skating," she admitted. "It was my first time living away from home, and I was eating dorm food, gaining weight, barely skating one session a day. Not sleeping properly at night . . . I know I'm missing out on college life right now, but I just can't afford that."

Michelle had only weeks to prepare for the world championships in Nice, France. She worked especially hard on her triple toe loop–triple toe loop combination. "This is a new generation of skaters," Michelle told *Sports Illustrated for Women*. "They're all doing triple-triples. I have to keep up. It comes to the point where you have to risk it. It can be the difference between first and second."

Despite her triple-triple, Michelle was in third place, behind Maria Butyrskaya and Irina Slutskaya, heading into the free skate in France. Just as she had been at the Olympics two years earlier, Michelle was the first skater in the last group. She knew what she had to do—skate clean and land all of her triple jumps. And that's just what she did. She landed seven triples, including a triple toe–triple toe combination that she had added to increase the difficulty of the program. Even though Michelle's marks were solid, 5.7s and 5.8s for technical merit and 5.8s and 5.9s for presentation, she was too nervous to watch her competitors skate. She knew the judges had still left room for another skater to win higher marks. She lay down backstage to stretch and try to forget about what was happening in the arena. On the ice, Russians Irina Slutskaya and Maria Butyrskaya didn't skate as well as Michelle. Butyrskaya didn't complete her combination jump and turned a triple salchow into a double while Slutskaya couldn't land either of her planned two combination jumps.

When it was all over, Michelle was the new world champion, with Irina in second and Maria in third. Michelle had fought her way back to win her third world championship title. It was an especially satisfying win for Michelle because she knew many people thought she had peaked and that she would never be the best in the world again with so many up-and-coming skaters at her heels. "I think that this is the most satisfying championship for me," Michelle told reporters. "There was a lot of pressure from the outside. 'You've got to do a triple-triple, got to do this, got to up the ante.'"

Michelle was named one of *People* magazine's "50 Most Beautiful People in the World" in 2000.

Over the summer, Michelle carefully reworked her schedule. She knew she needed to cut back on her course load, which meant it might take her six or seven years to graduate instead of the usual four. But she decided it was worth it. She wanted to skate and get her college degree. She took a full course load in the summer of 2000 and then chose classes that met in the early afternoons in the fall and winter terms so she could train three times a day. She also knew she'd have to take time off leading up to the 2002 Olympics so that she could devote her full attention to training.

In the fall, Michelle was up each day by seven and was on the ice before nine. She studied after her first practice until her second, which ended by noon. Then it was off to campus for class and back to the rink by late afternoon for her last session. Nighttime was for studying, e-mailing friends, and getting to bed early.

❝Sometimes school can be a nice distraction from skating, breaking up the day. Sometimes skating can be a nice distraction from school.❞

—MICHELLE KWAN

It was a regimented life, but all of her discipline and hard work was paying off. Michelle's new routines for the 2000–2001 season were her most difficult to date. She had harder triple combinations. She continued using a range of musical selections, with a jazz- and blues-influenced short program of pieces by Eric Clapton. She was especially proud of her long program, set to music called *Song of the Black Swan*. Michelle said, "Each season, I want to set challenges for myself. With seven triples, including a triple toe–triple toe combination, this program really challenged me to focus and maintain my speed."

Michelle took her new programs to Skate America and Skate Canada, where she came in first and second. (Irina Slutskaya finished first at Skate Canada.)

In October 2001, Michelle had to reschedule a midterm because she was competing in Skate America. She asked the professor if she needed to bring a note to prove she was going to be at the event. "I'll just watch it on TV," he said. "If I don't see you, then I'll know I've been had."

Soon it was time to travel to Boston for another national championship. Younger skaters Sarah Hughes and Sasha Cohen, who hadn't been much of a threat to Michelle several years earlier, had become legitimate rivals. Although Cohen wasn't at nationals because of an injury, she was known for her flexibility and artistry. Hughes was a great technician and getting better. But Michelle was still in a class all her own. One reporter called her routines the best since the 1998 nationals.

She earned seven 6.0s in her short program and two more in her long. She took home the gold and her fifth U.S. championship, giving her as many national titles as legendary figure skater Peggy Fleming.

In March, Michelle traveled to Vancouver, Canada, for the world championships, where she was considered the underdog and Irina Slutskaya was the favorite. Michelle was determined to win her fourth world championship crown. After finding herself second to Slutskaya after the short program, she skated a fantastic free skate and nailed her triple-triple. This performance proved once again that when she was skating well, Michelle was hard to beat. She won the competition.

Despite the difficulties of juggling school and skating, Michelle seemed to strike a good balance between the two. But as soon as she got used to being on campus or on the ice, it was another Olympic year and time for Michelle to put school on hold and prepare for another shot at Olympic gold.

Chapter | Ten

On Her Own

Michelle began the 2001–2002 season with a mixture of excitement and anxiety. She was ready for a change—she let Lori Nichol go as her choreographer and brought in Sarah Kawahara to work on her new long program. This time the Olympics were being held in the United States, in Salt Lake City, Utah. A gold medal win on her home turf would be perfect, but Michelle tried not to get ahead of herself. She needed to focus on training, so she temporarily moved back to Lake Arrowhead to train at Ice Castle. But something just didn't feel right to Michelle.

She struggled in competitions early in the season. Her skating lacked its usual spark. In mid-October, after a competition in which she gave an uninspired performance, Frank arranged an extra session so the two could work on improving her programs. Michelle called Frank the next day to say she'd like to train alone the following day and maybe the rest of the week. When

Michelle saw Frank at the rink at the end of the week, she was in tears. She told him she wanted to train alone all the time. Frank was stunned by the news. The two had had their differences in the past, but they had always worked things out. Still, Michelle felt this was the right decision for her, despite the fact that the Olympic Games would be held in less than four months. "It may be very close to the Olympics, but I think you have to believe and stick to your guns," Michelle explained to reporters. "I love Frank very much. Right now, it's just the decision I've made. We still care for each other, so it's not like it's the end of our relationship. It was a great ten years."

❝She really has a strong, strong feeling that she needs to do this by herself. That she has to be strong enough to go out there and lay it on the line without depending on me or depending on her father. That if she is to succeed, she has to be strong enough to do it herself.❞

—FRANK CARROLL,
AFTER MICHELLE LET HIM GO AS HER COACH

The media continued to wonder what was behind Michelle's decision, trying to determine if there was an underlying reason for the split that she wasn't revealing. Some wondered whether Michelle didn't want to train as hard as she used to. She was twenty-one years old, with a college career and a boyfriend, defenseman Brad Ference of the Florida Panthers hockey team. Michelle claimed the split had nothing to do with anyone but herself. "When I was younger, the coach was pretty much the skater. You did whatever he said. As I've gotten older, I've gotten more independent and I think for myself. That's the way it should be. . . . You have your differences in the way you should go about things, and that's what Frank and I ran into. I am very opinionated and so is Frank. I think I'm very hardheaded."

Despite the fact that he was no longer her coach, Frank had nothing but kind words for Michelle. He said: "Whether I'm with her or not, I want her to win. I think she's the best skater in the world." He wanted Michelle to find a new coach for her Olympic year, but Michelle didn't. Instead she scrapped the new short program she had been working on with Frank and decided to resurrect the Rachmaninoff short program she had skated so brilliantly at Nagano. She also decided to bring her father with her to the season's competitions. Although he wasn't acting as her coach, Danny sat with his daughter at each competition in the kiss-and-cry area as her scores were announced.

Fans and the media wondered whether Michelle's unusual training decisions would ruin her chance at an Olympic gold medal. But Michelle was undeterred. "There's a lot of things I've learned from 1998. After '98, you come to realize that the

Olympics isn't everything, it isn't your life. That six minutes on the ice, you can't justify it like that. After all the years and all the hard work, you've got to enjoy the process, not just the Olympics. If this is going to be my last Olympics—and I don't know if it is—you've got to cherish every moment."

❝I wouldn't be out here in the cold three times a day if I didn't care. I stayed eligible for the Olympics because I do care. I like the pressure. I like being pushed.❞

—MICHELLE KWAN

Michelle definitely cherished winning her sixth national title in early 2002 and earning her spot on the Olympic team. Unlike her competitors, Michelle didn't have a triple-triple combination, but the judges didn't seem to care. She landed all her other jumps cleanly and her footwork and two spread eagles dazzled the audience. She was awarded two 6.0s for presentation—bringing her all-time total perfect score count at nationals to a record twenty-seven! Sasha Cohen and Sarah Hughes placed second and third at nationals. They would join Michelle in representing the United States at the games. They, along with Russia's Irina Slutskaya, were expected to be Michelle's biggest competition for the gold medal. Michelle knew the pressure was on, but she decided not to get too worked up. This time she decided to stay in the Olympic village with the other athletes and attend other events that she had missed in 1998 because she was resting or training. She was in it for fun, not just for a shot at a gold medal.

OLYMPIC SCANDAL

The biggest figure skating news from the 2002 Olympics came from the pairs competition. The Russian pair of Yelena Berezhnaya and Anton Sikharulidze beat the Canadian pair of Jamie Sale and David Pelletier, even though many thought the Canadians had performed a much better program. Afterward, a French judge admitted that other judges had pressured her to vote for the Russians. In the end, the Russians were allowed to keep their gold, but in a special ceremony, the Canadians were presented with their own set of gold medals.

The gold medal seemed more of a reality the night of the ladies' short program, however. When Michelle took the ice, the crowd was already on its feet. She was shocked because she hadn't even skated yet. Their enthusiasm seemed to transfer to her and Michelle skated a great program. "I just let it all go," she said. "It's not worth holding back because I've seen what can happen. I just have to stick to the same thing in the long program." Heading into the long program, Michelle was in first place, followed by Irina, Sasha, and Sarah.

On February 21, 2002, the night of the free skate, Michelle was to skate second to last, after Sasha and Sarah but before Irina. She was ready. So was Sarah Hughes. The sixteen-year-old was in fourth place and didn't expect to win any color medal. She skated like she had nothing to lose. Her enthusiasm infected the crowd, who was cheering her on. In addition to her flow and grace on the ice, Sarah landed two triple-triple combinations, including the difficult triple salchow–triple loop combo. Her scores were mostly 5.7s and 5.8s. There was room for Michelle to pass her.

But Michelle struggled during her long program. She was unable to complete her triple toe–triple toe at the beginning of the program and turned the second jump into a double. Then, two minutes into the routine, she fell on her triple flip. The crowd rallied behind Michelle. She finished her routine but was clearly upset with the way she had skated. As she left the ice, Michelle covered her head to avoid getting pelted with all the stuffed animals raining down on her from the stands. When she made it to her father's side in the kiss-and-cry area, Michelle lightly punched the seat with her hand. The only way to win was if Irina had a disastrous free skate.

Irina encountered difficulties as well, but she didn't have as hard a time as Michelle. In the end, Sarah was the only skater to perform a clean program that evening, and she was able to climb from fourth all the way to first. Irina won the silver and Michelle the bronze. Once again the American national anthem played and once again Michelle, who had been the leader after the short program, had been beaten by a younger, less-experienced skater. She had every color Olympic medal except gold.

Even though she was crushed by her loss, Michelle was still the picture of grace and sportsmanship. She fought back tears as she spoke with reporters afterward. "I didn't skate very well," she admitted. "But I have to shrug my shoulders and go on." She congratulated Sarah, who was a huge fan of Michelle. One month later at worlds, Michelle struggled with her jump landings and finished second to Irina Slutskaya. Sarah did not compete, though she and Michelle were soon together again on the John Hancock Champions on Ice 2002 Olympic tour. During the four-month tour Michelle was still the crowd favorite. Fans admired both her skills and her attitude.

Fans sent more e-mail messages through the Olympic athletes' Web site to Michelle than to any other Olympic competitor. She received more than 1,800 messages from fans around the world.

Reporters wanted to know whether or not Michelle would turn professional and no longer compete at the more intense amateur level, where her competition was becoming younger and more nimble. Had the 2002 games been her last Olympics? "The tour is so long that it's giving me a chance to be able to tell what I want to do and how much I want to do. I know that I still enjoy competing," Michelle said. "It would be nice if I went back to school and did some other stuff, too. But I certainly don't think I'm going to say, 'OK, professional is the way to go.'"

---

66 *When you hang in there all these years, it can be hard to find the hunger. I have to find the spark inside me and turn on the switch.* 99

—MICHELLE KWAN

Soon Michelle was back to her training sessions and life in California. "The last few months I had just been training and training. I put school on hold. I pretty much put all ideas on hold. Seriously! There was no life after the 2002 Olympics as far as I was concerned. Now it's like, 'Oh, I kinda lost,' you know? So I'm starting to plan things." And first on Michelle's list of future plans? More skating!

Chapter | Eleven

Skating for Joy

In the spring of 2002, Michelle received the prestigious Sullivan Award at the New York Athletic Club as the top amateur athlete of 2001. She joined fellow figure skater and skating commentator Dick Button as the only skaters to have received the award. "It feels like a dream come true," she said.

That summer, Michelle turned twenty-two. She may have still been young, but she was much older than most of the skaters she was competing against. She found herself up against younger skaters who were doing more difficult jumps and jump combinations. When Michelle had become a senior ten years earlier, she had done more triple jumps than any of her competitors, but she had created some unexpected consequences. She was forced to scramble to keep up with a new generation of competitors. Even though she was one of the best skaters in the world, Michelle felt her skating was getting stale and needed to be reenergized. Although she had enjoyed not having a coach, relying on her own instincts, and making her own decisions, she missed having a second, trusted opinion when she was out on the ice.

❝*Michelle's a tiger underneath. She's a great fighter, a great competitor. She has a really passive outside and she's really easygoing. Everybody loves her and she's a great girl. But at the same time there's this real warrior inside that wants to accomplish these things.*❞

—BRIAN BOITANO

Michelle had known thirty-seven-year-old former skater Scott Williams for years, and she asked him if he'd like to coach her. Scott was one of the top men's skaters in the mid-1980s and had gone on to choreograph and direct ice shows as well as coach skaters like Amber Corwin and Tiffany and Johnny Steigler.

The pair agreed that their relationship would be more informal than a typical coaching one in which the coach makes most of the decisions. It would also not be as structured. They didn't have a set number of sessions each day, with Scott present at each one. "Michelle is very much in charge," Scott said. "She knows what she wants." Although Michelle trained every day, she took classes as well. At first she didn't commit to any of the season's big competitions, including nationals and worlds.

❝Skating is a huge chunk of my life, but the rest is just as important. Skating is not going to keep you company. It's not going to make you laugh. The ice doesn't talk back to you.❞

—MICHELLE KWAN

Michelle decided it was time to stop worrying about the competition. "I'm in a different stage of my life, and I'm not going to compare myself to anyone. I'm just going out there for my own good. And it feels good because I'm there for myself, and it should always be like that," she said. Michelle's new, more relaxed, go-with-the-flow attitude helped her have a stellar 2002–2003 season.

She skated at the Campbell's International Skating Classic and debuted her stunning new long program to the music *Concierto de Aranjuez,* composed by Spaniard Joaquin Rodrigo, and won the event. Although Michelle had decided not to attend Skate America in Spokane, Washington, she changed her mind after the USFSA asked her to reconsider. Many of the big-name skaters had dropped out of the event due to various injuries, and the event was suffering as a result. So Michelle made the trip and debuted her new short program to Peter Gabriel's "The

Feeling Begins." Because she didn't even have time to get a costume made, Michelle wore a gold costume she had used on tour. Despite the last-minute preparations, Michelle took home her seventh Skate America gold medal.

With two of a possible two wins for the season, Michelle decided to go to nationals in Dallas, Texas, in January 2003 and see if luck was still on her side. "I've been the favorite, the underdog, the little jumping bean. I've been everything," Michelle told reporters before the competition. "I've definitely had my ups and downs at nationals, but I feel mentally and physically prepared this time. I'm nervous, of course. . . . I'm human."

66 *It's exhilarating to see the pure joy with which [Michelle] skates when she's at her best. She reaches every person in the audience, even in the last row of bleachers. She skates from her soul.* 99

—JESSICA BUSSGANG, TOP U.S. SKATING JUDGE

But she had little reason to worry. Michelle had two clean skates and earned mostly 5.9s and even a 6.0 for presentation as she won her sixth consecutive national title and her seventh overall. In her long program, a reenergized Michelle had three triple jumps in three minutes and intricate footwork that was reminiscent of flamenco dancing. She left her competitors Sarah and

Sasha behind with her full, mature skating style. "It takes years to get there," explained commentator and former champion Peggy Fleming. "The meaning of everything is a little different as you get older. It's a nice feeling to physically express that on ice."

After the win at nationals, little question remained about whether she would compete at worlds. After all, they were being held in Washington, D.C. "Worlds being here is exciting, so it's kind of like a little teaser," she said. "I want to be there." Even though she didn't have a triple-triple combination in her program, Michelle proved that she was still at the top of her game and the best in the world. She didn't need a triple-triple jump combination to earn three 6.0s. There was even a new, temporary judging system in place for the event that many were criticizing. After a judging scandal in the 2002 Olympic pairs event, the scoring system for skating was closely examined. The interim judging system in place for the 2002–2003 season used a computer to randomly select nine of the fourteen judges' marks so that no one country's skater could be favored.

But Michelle had nothing on her mind that night except skating a clean program. Her biggest problem was that she could hardly hear her music over the roars of the crowd. Michelle still kept time to it beautifully. In the last thirty seconds of her long program, Michelle began her routine's straight line footwork that *Sports Illustrated* skating writer E. M. Swift called "an exquisite, [Fred] Astaire-like dance of exuberance that was more like a scene of great theater than sport." The 16,116 people in attendance at the MCI Center were on their feet before Michelle finished. "I've never felt such energy from myself," Michelle later said. "It tells me I should put less pressure on myself and just go out and have fun. That's how it should have been last year." Michelle's fifth world title tied her with Carol Heiss Jenkins for the most world crowns won by an American skater. "It's pretty amazing," Michelle admitted. "I have no words. I don't know what to think."

❛❛*I think in twenty years, we'll look back on Michelle Kwan as one of the most remarkable athletes in history—whether or not she ever wins an Olympic gold medal.*❜❜
—PEGGY FLEMING, U.S. OLYMPIC FIGURE SKATING GOLD MEDALIST AND SPORTS COMMENTATOR

Michelle spent her summer touring with Champions on Ice before settling in for another season of skating. She planned to continue competing and going to classes and is considering majoring in psychology. But as Michelle began the 2003–2004 season, she seemed to be missing some of the passion and fire she'd shown at the end of the previous season. At her first competition—the Campbell's International Figure Skating Classic in early October—

she unveiled a brand-new long program to Puccini's opera *Tosca*, but finished in second to elegant Sasha Cohen. Fortunately, Michelle no longer had to fight off challenges from Sarah Hughes, who was a full-time college student in her first year at Yale.

❝*Medals are just medals. It's [about] the performance and the love for skating and the feeling I have when I am out there in front of a crowd.***❞**

—MICHELLE KWAN

In late November, Michelle decided she needed to take a more challenging approach to her training. She hired a new coach, former Russian skater and jump technician Rafael Arutunian. Just two weeks after making the switch, Michelle beat Sasha to win the International Figure Skating Challenge.

At the U.S. nationals, held in Atlanta, Georgia, in early January 2004, the pressure was on. Michelle used the same short program she'd used at the 2003 nationals. She had a slight bobble on the landing of her double axel, putting her in second place behind Sasha. In the long program, Michelle seemed to embody the drama of *Tosca*. She showed unwavering confidence, landing each jump solidly and drawing in the audience with her intensity. As had happened at the 2003 worlds, the audience rose to a standing ovation long before she had finished the program. Her footwork sequence in the last moments of the program resembled a joyous victory lap around the rink. Afterward, her fans shouted, "six, six," and the judges agreed, awarding her seven perfect 6.0s for presentation. Once again, Michelle had proved that when she was at her best, she was unbeatable. Her next challenge would come in late March, at the world championships in Dortmund, Germany. Rafael Arutunian indicated that he'd be working with Michelle in the meantime to increase the difficulty of her long program, adding a triple-triple combination. He also hinted that he had a plan to prepare her for the 2006 Olympics.

Estimates have Michelle's endorsement income at $2 million a year.

Despite having a stunning five world championship titles and eight national championship titles, Michelle doesn't seem ready to retire from the amateur ranks anytime soon. "I can't imagine [turning] professional," she said. "I enjoy pushing myself. I enjoy competing. Why should I stop doing what I love?"

A Decade of Brilliance

More than a decade has passed since Michelle started competing at the senior level, and the USFSA honored her for her achievements in 2003. At a banquet during a meeting in Norfolk, Virginia, guests celebrated a "Decade of Brilliance" with Michelle. Her spectacular career was chronicled with video highlights that included messages from her Champions on Ice castmates as well as her free skate at the 2003 world championships.

Michelle gave a speech in which she thanked the USFSA, her family, friends, and fellow skaters. "Even though skating is an individual sport, I think of it as a team sport," she said to the crowd. Michelle didn't even try to stop the tears from falling on that special night.

After Michelle's win at the 2004 nationals, many wondered if she would ever win the elusive Olympic gold. Would she try again in Turin, Italy, in 2006 when she will be twenty-five years old? Michelle isn't ruling anything out—she calls her chances for being in Turin "pretty high."

She may very well be at the top of the medals podium at the Olympics one day, but if she is never there, she won't be broken-hearted. She has accomplished more than she ever dreamed when she first laced up her rental skates as a little girl. And in doing so, she captured the attention and the hearts of skating fans around the world, who couldn't help but be touched by Michelle's ups and downs. More than any other skater in history, she seems to have a fan base that just keeps growing as her career continues.

When asked how it feels to be a skating icon, Michelle admitted that she still feels like she's living in a bubble and can't exactly say. But she feels she has touched people through her skating, which is what she has always wanted to do. She said in one of her books, "People sometimes ask me what I want my lasting impact on figure skating to be. I want to be more than someone who did a lot of triples. When people think of me, I'd like them to remember an emotion—the way they felt when they watched me skate. If I can give them a memory of that happiness, that is more than I could ever hope for. And if I can always have the happiness that skating brings me, it would be a dream come true."

CAREER STATS

Year	Competition	Finish
1993	United States Championships	Sixth
1994	United States Championships	Second
1994	World Championships	Eighth
1995	United States Championships	Second
1995	World Championships	Fourth
1996	United States Championships	First
1996	World Championships	First
1997	United States Championships	Second
1997	World Championships	Second
1998	United States Championships	First
1998	Olympic Games	Second
1998	World Championships	First
1999	United States Championships	First
1999	World Championships	Second
2000	United States Championships	First
2000	World Championships	First
2001	United States Championships	First
2001	World Championships	First
2002	United States Championships	First
2002	Olympic Games	Third
2002	World Championships	Second
2003	United States Championships	First
2003	World Championships	First
2004	United States Championships	First

GLOSSARY

axel jump: a jump in which the skater takes off forward from one foot and spins in the air to land on the other foot going backward. Most female skaters do a double axel (which is actually two-and-a-half revolutions), while male skaters often do triples.

butterfly: a pretty move skaters often save for the end of their programs in which a skater's body rotates horizontally over the ice while her legs whirl behind her like a butterfly's wings.

combination: two or more jumps in a row. As soon as the first jump is landed, a skater starts performing the second.

edge: the outside or inside of a skating blade.

flip jump: a jump in which a skater pushes off the back inside edge of the skate while digging the toe pick of the opposite foot into the ice and lands on the picking foot.

footwork: a required element that involves fast, connected steps across the surface of the ice. Points are deducted if a skater's footwork is sloppy or does not cover the ice.

long program: also called the free skate. It features a skater's artistic or creative moves, and there are no required elements. For women, the long program is four minutes long and for men, four and a half minutes.

loop jump: a jump that begins on the back outside edge of a skater's blade and ends with a landing on the same back outside edge. If the skater uses a toe pick to get started in the revolutions, the jump is called a toe loop.

lutz jump: a jump in which a skater takes off from a back outside edge, using the toe pick of the opposite foot to launch into the air, and lands on the back outside edge of the picking foot.

salchow jump: a jump that starts off the back inside edge and ends on the back outside edge of the other foot.

short program: this two-and-a-half-minute routine calls on the skater to perform eight required elements in any order the skater chooses.

spiral: a move that shows off control, speed, and flexibility. A skater extends one leg behind as high as it can go and glides across the ice with all of the weight on the inside or outside edge of the other skate.

spread eagle: a move in which the skater's legs are spread, heels facing each other and toes pointing straight out, while gliding in an arc around the ice.

toe pick: the small, jagged teeth on the front of the figure skate blade.

SOURCES

1   Kwan, Michelle, as told to Laura
    James, *Heart of a Champion* (New
    York: Scholastic, 1997), 150.
7   Ibid., 15.
7   Kwan, Michelle, *My Special
    Moments* (New York: Hyperion,
    2001), 19.
9   Kwan, Michelle, as told to Laura
    James, *The Winning Attitude!: What
    It Takes to Be a Champion* (New
    York: Hyperion, 1999), 3–4.
10 Kwan, Michelle, *Heart of a
    Champion*, 23.
11 Kwan, Michelle, *My Special
    Moments*, 42.
13 Kwan, Michelle, *Heart of a
    Champion*, 28.
13 Herr, Laurie, "Meet Michelle,"
    Winner, November 1997, 10.
14–15 Kwan, Michelle, *The Winning
    Attitude!*, 27.
17 Kwan, Michelle, *Heart of a
    Champion*, 37.
18 Ibid., 42.
18 Kwan, Michelle, *My Special
    Moments*, 45.
19 Kwan, Michelle, *The Winning
    Attitude!*, 87–88.
20 Kwan, Michelle, *Heart of a
    Champion*, 43.
20 Starr, Mark, "Kwan Song,"
    Newsweek, February 18, 2002, 50.
21 Kwan, Michelle, *The Winning
    Attitude!*, ix.
24 Kwan, Michelle, *Heart of a
    Champion*, 49–50.
24 Ibid., 64.
25 Ibid., 53.
28 Bondy, Filip, "Seeking a Perfect 6 At
    a Precocious 12," *New York Times*,
    January 21, 1993, B13.
29 Kwan, Michelle, *Heart of a
    Champion*, 64.
33 Ibid., 68.
34 Ibid., 65.
35 Ibid., 72.
37 Kwan, Michelle, *My Special
    Moments*, 7.

38 Becker, Debbie, "Michelle Kwan,
    14, top U.S. hope for '98 Olympic
    gold," *Chinatown News*, March 18,
    1995, 8.
38 Longman, Jere, "For Bobek, the
    Desire Translates Into a Title," *New
    York Times*, February 12, 1995, S3.
39 Clarey, Christopher, "After Some
    False Starts, Bobek Glides to the
    Top," *New York Times*, March 11,
    1995, 35.
39 Clarey, Christopher, "Chinese Skater
    Glides to World Title as Bobek Falls
    to the Bronze," *New York Times*,
    March 12, 1995, S4.
40 Becker, Debbie, "Michelle Kwan,
    14, top U.S. hope for '98 Olympic
    gold," *Chinatown News*, March 18,
    1995, 8.
40 Kwan, Michelle, *Heart of a
    Champion*, 92–93.
41 Longman, Jere, "Grace and
    Improvisation: Kwan Wins World
    Title," *New York Times*, March 24,
    1996, S1.
41 Longman, Jere, "Eldredge
    Impressive; Kwan Breaks Through,"
    New York Times, October 30, 1995,
    C10.
42 Davis, David, "Lord of the Rink,"
    Los Angeles Magazine, January
    2002, 30.
44 Longman, Jere, "Kwan Leads, with
    Polish and Poise," *New York Times*,
    January 20, 1996, 33.
45 Longman, Jere, "Grace and
    Improvisation: Kwan Wins World
    Title," *New York Times*, March 24,
    1996, S1.
46 Ibid.
47 Kwan, Michelle, *Heart of a
    Champion*, 106.
47 Ibid., 82.
48 Ibid., photo insert.
50 Ibid., 113.
51 Ibid., 122.
52 Swift, E.M., "Into the Light," *Sports
    Illustrated*, February 9, 1998, 114.

53 Kwan, Michelle, *The Winning Attitude!*, 114.

54 Longman, Jere, "Kwan's Spills Open Door For a Younger Champion," *New York Times*, February 16, 1997, S1.

55 Longman, Jere, "Kwan Overcomes Jitters With Grace As Bobek Stumbles," *New York Times*, February 15, 1997, 31.

56 Longman, Jere, "When Maturity Is the Enemy," *New York Times*, March 16, 1997, B11.

57 Kwan, Michelle, *My Special Moments*, 42.

57 Longman, Jere, "Lipinski, 14, Is Youngest World Champion," *New York Times*, March 23, 1997, S5.

58 Kwan, Michelle, *My Special Moments*, 6.

59 Swift, E.M., "Into the Light," 114.

60 Ibid.

62 Ibid.

63 Kwan, Michelle, *Heart of a Champion*, 156.

65–66 Phillips, Bob, "Graceful Kwan still seeking gold," *ESPN.com*, n.d., <http://espn.go.com/classic /biography/s/Kwan_Michelle.html> (November 17, 2003).

66 Ibid.

66 Kwan, Michelle, *Heart of a Champion*, 159.

68 Swift, E.M., "Kwan's Song," *Sports Illustrated for Women*, Jan/Feb 2001, 56.

71 "Despite Falling, Kwan Gets Third Title," *New York Times*, February 14, 1999, SP3.

72 Clarey, Christopher, "A Tumble Puts Kwan in Fourth At Worlds," *New York Times*, March 29, 1999, D4.

73 Paprocki, Sherry Beck, *Michelle Kwan* (Philadelphia: Chelsea House Publishers, 2001), 59.

73 Kwan, Michelle, *My Special Moments*, 9.

73 Longman, Jere, "Kwan Finds Artistry Battling Athleticism," *New York Times*, February 10, 2000, D4.

74–75 Swift, E.M., "Kwan's Song," 56.

75 Ibid.

76 Clarey, Christopher, "Kwan Battles Back To Win Her Third Title," *New York Times*, April 2, 2000, SP12.

77 Swift, E.M., "Kwan's Song," 56.

78 Kwan, Michelle, *My Special Moments*, 12.

78 Swift, E.M., "Kwan's Song," 56.

81 March, Lyndsey, "Kwan Splits with Coach Frank Carroll," *iskater.com*, October 23, 2001, <http://iskater .com/headlines/archive/ 2001october/kwancarroll.htm> (July 20, 2003).

81 Associated Press, "Kwan says she's going to direct her own career," *ESPN.com*, October 23, 2001, <http://espn.go.com/skating/news /2001/1023/1267912.html> (November 26, 2003).

82 March, Lyndsey, "Kwan Splits with Coach Frank Carroll," *iskater.com*, October 23, 2001, <http://iskater .com/headlines/archive/2001october /kwancarroll.htm> (July 20, 2003).

82 Ibid.

82–83 Niyo, John, "Kwan Relies on Herself to Weather Tumultuous Year," *Detnews.com*, December 7, 2001, <http://www.detnews.com/2001/ moresports/0112/07/h03-361501 .htm> (November 26, 2003).

83 Swift, E.M., "Kwan's Song," 56.

84–85 Michaelis, Vicki, "Kwan out to have fun this time around," *USA Today*, February 20, 2002, 03d.

86 Michaelis, Vicki, "Kwan undecided about '06 games," *USA Today*, February 22, 2002, 03d.

87 Michaelis, Vicki, "Kwan not pro yet, mulling over 2006 Olympics bid," *USAToday.com*, April 4, 2002, <http://www.usatoday.com/sports /olympics/winter/2002–04-04 -kwan.htm> (November 26, 2003).

87 Starr, Mark, "Michelle's Next Turn," *Newsweek*, March 26, 2001, 46.

87 Yu, Ting, "Pop Quiz with Michelle Kwan," *People*, April 8, 2002, 24.

88 Cronin, Don, "Kwan Wins Sullivan Award," *USA Today*, April 10, 2002, 01c.

89 Phillips, Bob, "Graceful Kwan still seeking gold," *ESPN.com,* n.d., <http://www.espn.go.com /classic/biography/s/Kwan _Michelle.html> (November 17, 2003).

89 "The 2002–03 Season: Michelle Kwan," *USFSA.org,* n.d., <http://www.usfsa.org/news/2002 –03/kwan-recap.htm> (November 26, 2003).

90 "Michelle Kwan," *Newsweek,* March 24, 2003, 67.

90 "The 2002–03 Season: Michelle Kwan," *USFSA.org,* n.d., <http://www.usfsa.org/news/2002 –03/kwan-recap.htm> (November 26, 2003).

91 Ibid.

91 Der, Bob, "Everything But the Gold," *Sports Illustrated for Kids,* February 2002, 29.

92 Roberts, Selena, "A Performance Beyond Youth's Flights of Fancy," *New York Times,* January 20, 2003, D3.

92 "The 2002–03 Season: Michelle Kwan," *USFSA.org,* n.d., <http://www.usfsa.org/news/2002 –03/kwan-recap.htm> (November 26, 2003).

93 Swift, E.M., "Kwan Do," *Sports Illustrated,* April 7, 2003, 24.

93 Ibid.

93 "The 2002–03 Season: Michelle Kwan," *USFSA.org,* n.d., <http://www.usfsa.org/news/2002 –03/kwan-recap.htm> (November 26, 2003).

93 2003 World Figure Skating Championships, ABC Sports, television broadcast March 29, 2003.

94 Cawley, Janet. "15 Extraordinary Women: Michelle Kwan," *Biography,* July 2002, 52.

95 Ibid.

96 "The 2002–03 Season: Michelle Kwan," *USFSA.org,* n.d., <http://www.usfsa.org/news/2002 –03/kwan-recap.htm> (November 26, 2003).

97 Brennan, Christine, "Kwan planning one more run at elusive Olympic gold medal," *USA Today,* January 7, 2004, C14.

97 Kwan, Michelle, *My Special Moments,* 43.

BIBLIOGRAPHY

Gatto, Kimberly. *Michelle Kwan: Champion on Ice.* Minneapolis, MN: Lerner Publications, 1998.

Kwan, Michelle. *My Special Moments.* New York: Hyperion, 2001.

Kwan, Michelle, as told to Laura James. *Heart of a Champion.* New York: Scholastic, 1997.

Kwan, Michelle, as told to Laura James. *The Winning Attitude!: What It Takes to Be a Champion.* New York: Hyperion, 1999.

Paprocki, Sherry Beck. *Michelle Kwan.* Philadelphia: Chelsea House Publishers, 2001.

Wilner, Barry. *Michelle Kwan: Star Figure Skater.* Berkeley Heights, NJ: Enslow Publishers, 2001.

WEB SITES

U.S. Figure Skating Online
www.usfsa.org
This official Web site of the United States Figure Skating Association features skaters' biographies, career statistics, and season highlights.

INDEX